AEROGRAMS ACROSS THE OCEAN

A LOVE STORY IN LETTERS

Aerograms Across the Ocean

A LOVE STORY IN LETTERS

RACHEL AND DAVID BIALE

WILDCAT BOOKS

Aerograms Across the Ocean

by Rachel and David Biale

ISBN 978-1-0880-1026-6

WILDCAT BOOKS

For our children, Noam and Tali, who have also found their true loves.

And in memory of our parents, Jacob and Evelyn Biale, Chaim and Anina Korati.

TABLE OF CONTENTS

LOVE IN THE TIME OF CORONA

WE WERE CHILDREN of a turbulent age, not unlike our own. It was the early 1970s. America was still stuck deep in the quagmire of the Vietnam War, while, at home, opposition to the war and movements for civil rights, women's rights and the counter-culture continued to gather steam. Many young Americans, especially in the universities, were deeply pessimistic about the country's future. Israel was still in the after-glow of the Six Day War, but the occupation of Palestinian lands in 1967 was becoming entrenched. Prospects of improved relations, let alone peace, with Arab countries and the Palestinians remained tenuous, with ominous hints of the coming catastrophe of the 1973 Yom Kippur War. The secular socialism of Israel's founders seemed to have entered a period of crisis, where the identity of the state was no longer taken for granted and the very meaning of being Jewish in Israel was contested. And, in America, the prevailing definition of Judaism as a religion seemed inadequate for those searching for deeper identification with Jewish history.

We were non-conformists, politically alienated from the directions in which our two countries were moving. We both faced the military draft and, while David was determined to avoid serving in the Vietnam War, Rachel was prepared to serve in Israel's army. We were intent on forging a Jewish identity that was not religious but still rooted in the Jewish literary tradition. For both of us, study of Jewish texts took the place of religious practice. We were deeply committed to the ideal of kibbutz, but dissatisfied with how that utopian experiment had lost much of its idealism and become conventional. We were also at odds with the cultural conformism of our countries of origin and attracted – albeit with reservations -- to the emerging counter-culture. We admired much in each other's country but also found much to criticize.

This memoir is based on 258 letters that we exchanged after meeting in Israel in the summer of 1970. The letters span the period from September 1970 to July 1972, when David was in Berkeley and Rachel in Israel (Rachel is referred to throughout as Racheli, the diminutive by which she is known to friends and family). The letters lay dormant for nearly fifty years in file folders perched on a side shelf. We would mention them to each other on occasion and also promised our children that they could read them once they got married. Our son, Noam, married Margaret in 2014, but the files didn't budge.

In the summer of 2018, David came across them while looking for something connected with his research. Wondering whether they would be embarrassing to read so long after we wrote them, he began to look through them. Surprised to find himself moved by much of what he read, he pressed Racheli to read them as well. She was occupied with other projects, and, she admitted, a bit wary of meeting herself as a very young, idealistic and occasionally self-important kibbutznik, as well as a romantically and sexually inexperienced girl, still not quite a woman.

Another opportunity presented itself as our daughter, Tali, and her partner, Willie, began to plan their wedding for August 2020. Perhaps now was the time for both of us to read the letters and pass them on to our children. However, the coronavirus pandemic postponed the wedding, which meant that the urgency faded again. But the epidemic also left us alone-together with many more hours to fill than in our normal busy lives. Covid's march of death across the world, raised for us – and for so many others – the specter of illness and mortality.

And, then, that specter visited us directly. In August 2020, David received a diagnosis of metastatic prostate cancer. Both of us were forced to think about the arc of our lives, of our accomplishments and struggles, joys and, yes, tragedies. If the future was no longer limitless (and, of course, it never was), we could at least return to the charmed chapter of our lives when we fell in love. After he learned of his diagnosis, David wrote a letter to Racheli on August 4, 2020 to commemorate fifty years since the day we first met. He concluded:

And, now that a half century is gone, here you are taking care of me on what we hope is not my final journey. We have done a lot in the last fifty years, you and I. An amazing family, a wonderful home, dear friends on three continents, many books and trips. And, above all, unending love, which must now be stronger than death.

Revisiting that period so long ago, when our journey first began, now seemed truly urgent. Racheli began to look at the letters and she, too, became quite obsessed. Since her letters were handwritten on onion-skin paper with the ink fading, she transcribed all of them and scanned all of David's letters, mostly typed on aerograms. She also translated the handful of letters we'd written in Hebrew.

Now, what, if anything, should we do with these letters besides share them with our kids? Our friend Fred Rosenbaum, after reading about half of the letters, proposed that we write a joint memoir, with generous quotations woven together by our own narrative. We had never encountered such a genre, so we decided to invent it as we went along. We organized the memoir according to the chronology of the letters, each of us writing entries keyed to the date of the letters. Unlike today's instantaneous communications, letters between California and Israel took an average of seven to ten days. At first, we waited to receive a letter before we answered it. But, soon enough, we were corresponding more frequently, which meant that letters were passing each other across the Atlantic. Like astronomers observing light emitted by a star many millions of years earlier, we were each responding to something that had already been superseded by a later letter. We chose to keep the original chronology of the letters so that readers could experience our epistolary relationship as we did.

Where we quoted from the letters, as opposed to paraphrasing or summarizing, we preserved the language of the letters, exactly as we wrote them (correcting on rare occasions small inaccuracies or ungrammatical constructions). We chose passages that we thought best reflected our romantic, philosophical and political views at the time. We took pains not to censor ourselves or each other. Occasionally, we reflected back from our present vantage point to provide some background on issues and events that were important to us at the time or to add information from later in our lives.

———————

It was now more than half a year into the coronavirus pandemic. The grave toll was ever-present, and yet, there was a moment in early November 2020 when it seemed reasonably safe to travel East and spend nearly a month with Noam, Margaret, our four-year old granddaughter Rosemary, and our new grandson, Abraham. That opportune moment was amplified by the good news that David was responding exceptionally well to his treatment and experiencing very few side effects. His doctor gave him the green light to travel.

Before joining Noam and his family in New Jersey, we quarantined in their apartment in Downtown Brooklyn (a week earlier they had gone to a rented house on the Jersey shore for the winter months).

We decided to turn the twelve days of isolation into a writers' retreat. Each of us began to compose our own sections of the memoir. Our writing became all-consuming: when we weren't eating, sleeping or taking a daily walk, we wrote obsessively. By the time we returned home to Berkeley in mid-December, we had a full draft of each of our sections. After a first round of editing independently, we read the whole manuscript out loud to each other. We generally agreed, sometimes argued, and occasionally teared up, stopping for an embrace.

Both of us are writers. David has written or edited eleven books in his field of Jewish history. Racheli has written more eclectically: an academic book, a memoir, a historical novel, and a parenting advice book. Writing has never been difficult for either of us and, over the years, has become an essential way in which we express ourselves. We have both known and cherished that surge of energy that comes from full-on engagement in a writing project. But nothing prepared us for this: it was a period of luminous intensity. The emotions aroused by this shared work were sweet and poignant, sharpened by the effects of months-long isolation in the shadow of lethal illness, both global and personal.

We knew how the story of those two tumultuous years of letter writing would end. Perhaps for that reason, we found that our rosy memories had partially obscured the angst of a relationship that developed almost entirely in letters. We couldn't help sometimes wishing that our younger selves might have had the benefit of hindsight. There were moments when we wanted to reach back, from the present to our long-ago selves, put a loving hand on our own shoulder and say, "It will work out just fine."

We were also moved, and at times bemused, by the passions, intellectual struggles, doubts and uncertainties of our youth. Today, these struggles and doubts have melted away, replaced by the conviction that we have lived the lives we were meant to live. As fraught as those years of letter writing were, we wouldn't want them to have been otherwise, since they gave us the gift of a dramatic romance and its written record. And, perhaps even more importantly, the process of writing has nourished our love beyond anything we could have asked for in these stormy times.

Prologue 1: Racheli

IT BEGAN WITH A BANG

IT BEGAN WITH A BANG. But not the kind you're thinking of: it was *under* the bed that it all started. It was the summer of 1970. I had just graduated high school and was spending the summer at home on the kibbutz preparing for the matriculation exams. My friend Navah Haber-Schaim had arrived at the kibbutz and had arranged for a guy she had met at the advanced Hebrew class at Ulpan Akiva in Netanyah to come work here as a volunteer. "This David," she had said on the phone, "is really into Jewish things. You'll have a lot to talk about. And his Hebrew is great, so he can work anywhere on the kibbutz where he's needed." There was something in her voice. I had a hunch she liked him, which primed me for romantic possibilities, too. It didn't take much at that age.

Indeed, the moment I met David, something stirred in me. But I don't think it was romance yet. Rather, he seemed to be the personification of my image of an American Jewish student, with his lanky torso and gold wire-rim glasses framing inquisitive eyes.

This was the kind of "boy" who had so impressed me at Newton High School the year my family spent in America. But could looks be deceiving? Once we started talking the answer was resounding: this *was* the type of young American Jewish intellectual I had in mind.

There was something about him that was unlike any of the young men I grew up with, especially those a few years older than me who had fought in the Six Day War, the swagger in the way they walked and the way they talked. We all honed a cynical disdain for the traditional kibbutz, first and foremost the emblematic *kova tembel* (literally "dunce's hat" – a round-rimmed cloth cap). We would wear anything else, but never a kova tembel. And there was David, on his first day of work as a volunteer at Kfar Ruppin, entering the kibbutz dining room, wearing one of them, and an unusually big one, at that. And he was proud of it! He explained it wasn't just any old kova tembel, but a "kova Shifra," hand-sewn by a relative, Shifra Harpaz, who was a venerable founder of Kibbutz Mishmar Ha-Emek, where he had scored the coveted hat. Half of me cringed. The other half marveled: he didn't seem to care what others thought of him, a quality I truly aspired to. And when he started talking about ideology and philosophy, topics most kibbutzniks my age sarcastically dismissed, there was a sparkle in his eyes which I had not seen in anyone else's, except occasionally... in my own.

I had warned Navah and asked her to make sure David realized this too: there were shellings of the kibbutz nearly every night. Most often it was three or four mortar shells lobbed at the kibbutz by the Palestine Liberation Organization from across the Jordan River. But occasionally they added the much more destructive Russian-made *Katyusha* rockets. On August 7, nearing 8:00 pm, the three of us – Navah, David and I -- were sitting in my parents' apartment doing just what Navah had promised: talking about "Jewish things." My parents had gone off to attend some kibbutz committee meetings. Suddenly we heard a piercing whistle and almost instantly, a thundering bang.

"Under the bed" I commanded, taking charge as the local expert. We dove under the bed in the living room, which served as a couch in daytime. We wriggled around in order to fit all essential body parts under the single bed.

"That was too close for us to run to the shelter," I explained as we tried to catch our breath on the cold tile floor. "It's too dangerous to run outside, because we'd have to run around the house to the shelter." They stared at me, clearly unable to say a word.

"We should be fine here," I said cheerily, trying to lift their spirits, "that is, as long as there isn't a direct hit on the house." I had to be accurate. Then the siren wailed, as usual, within a minute of the first shell exploding.

"There," I said, "that's the kibbutz siren. But we don't really need it, do we?"

Navah and David remained silent. I tried to pick up the conversation where we'd left off, while we heard two more screeching whistles and explosions shook the house. The conversation dead-ended. I switched to jokes, which weren't terribly successful either but, thankfully, now the explosions seemed further away. Soon we heard distant rumblings.

"Ah, that's good," I perked up, "that's the IDF shelling them back. This will be over soon." Indeed, about ten minutes later we heard the kibbutz siren again, this time signaling the All Clear. When it was bedtime, Navah and I went to my room and David to his. I don't believe he slept at all that night.

And that is how our love began, although it took a long time and many letters, some of which you'll read here, to get out from *under* the bed ... and *onto* it.

Prologue 2: David

BETWEEN TWO PROMISED LANDS

IT WAS AUGUST 4, 1970 and, even though I didn't know it then, it was the most important day of my life. I took the bus from Tel Aviv to Afula and then from Afula to the dusty little town of Beit She'an. I waited in the sun that beat down on my head like a hammer on an anvil until the bus to Kibbutz Kfar Ruppin picked me up. We descended into the valley – more than 200 meters below sea level – where the heat was, if anything, even more unrelenting. At 4:00 pm, the bus entered the gates of the kibbutz.

Someone directed me to the house of Hanna Ilsar, the veteran kibbutz member in charge of volunteers. Hanna, who was one of the German Jews who founded the kibbutz in 1938, spoke a garbled Hebrew rather worse than my own. But I understood her directions to the apartment of the Korati family. I walked there and entered the wrong door: the bedroom instead of the living room. That's where it all began.

But how, or better, *why* did I get there? I suppose I should start with my father Jacob's story, since, in a sense, I was following circuitously in his footsteps. Born in Wloclawek, Poland in 1908, his parents were religious but already beginning to flirt with modernity. His father, Avraham Yosef, a leather merchant, was the follower of a Hasidic rabbi, but also belonged to Mizrahi, the religious Zionist party. He was something of a *maskil*, an enlightened Jew, who read the poet Hayim Nahman Bialik, already crowned the "Hebrew national poet." Avraham also helped found a modern Hebrew gymnasium in the town. My father's mother, Bracha, was the first Jewish woman in the town to throw off the *sheitel* (the wig worn by married Orthodox Jewish women) and let her own hair grow, a gesture of modernizing and perhaps incipient Jewish feminism.

My father and his two siblings revolted against their moderately traditional parents in the mode of many young Polish Jews between the wars. He and his sister Frania joined Hashomer Hatzair, the radical socialist Zionist youth movement; his brother David joined Betar, the militant rightwing Zionist movement. My father's most formative experience was between the ages of sixteen and twenty in Hashomer Hatzair from 1924 to 1928. He and his comrades insisted on speaking Hebrew to each other and bonded on long hikes in the Polish countryside. He became a group leader and a picture of him in that role shows him surrounded by a bevy of dreamy-eyed Hashomer girls. With his comrades, he dreamt of living in Eretz Israel (Mandatory Palestine at the time) and working the land on a kibbutz. In fact, those under my father's tutelage went to Kibbutz Negba in the Negev desert where, two decades later, they heroically held off the invading Egyptian army.

They planned to be "scientific farmers," so some of them first went to study modern agricultural methods. Because my father had relatives in the San Francisco Bay Area, he journeyed in 1928 from Poland to the University of California, Berkeley. He knew no English and was able to communicate with his chemistry professor in German. By the spring, however, he was already writing flawless

Hashomer Hatzair Group September, 1928

English. His advisers at Berkeley told him that if he really wanted to study hands-on agriculture, he had to go to the "University Farm" at Davis, seventy miles northeast of Berkeley. As it turned out, exactly seventy years later, I would join the History Department faculty at Davis, by now a full-fledged campus of the University of California.

At Davis, my father studied pruning, irrigation and other farming skills. After an eighteen-month stint in the dry, dusty Central Valley of California, he returned to Berkeley to complete a bachelor's degree in 1931. His plan was to go to Palestine as soon as he received a "certificate" (an entry visa) from the British authorities. For months, he waited for the precious document, but, meanwhile, he was offered a fellowship to do a PhD in plant physiology. He accepted it and started his program, only to receive the certificate a few months later. It was too late; he had already embarked on what would be his life's work. It was one of those tricks of timing that can change the course of everything that follows.

In 1934, PhD in hand, he returned to Poland to visit his family for what would be, unbeknownst to all of them, the last time. During that summer visit, he married a woman named Kala, who had been one of his comrades in the youth movement. He returned to the US intent on getting her a visa, but the Immigration Service challenged his citizenship, threatening him with deportation to Poland. The case dragged on in the courts for four years until he was vindicated, but, meanwhile, Kala had lost hope, asked him for a divorce, married another man, had a child ... and she and her family perished in the Holocaust. This was a secret that my father took to the grave. After he died, I discovered the letters he and Kala wrote each other in the file cabinet in his office at UCLA.

There was no academic employment in the US during the Great Depression, so he apparently seriously entertained a position in the Soviet Union, which would have been a disastrous career move just two years before the Great Purge. Fortunately, at the last minute, the United Fruit Company gave the UCLA Department of Agriculture a $5,000 grant to find out why fruit was going moldy in transit. Nobody wanted to work on it, so they hired my father for one year. He stayed for fifty-five.

By the time of World War II, he was already a faculty member at UCLA, but he was deeply worried about his family in Nazi-occupied Poland. His younger brother, for whom I'm named, had died three weeks into the war as a soldier in the Polish army. His parents were incarcerated in the Warsaw Ghetto where his father died of typhus. His mother was most probably murdered in Treblinka. Although he knew only fragments of this story (and would learn the rest only after the war), he was highly motivated to fight. His years in the youth movement had turned him into a great outdoorsman. He hiked and skied the Sierra Nevada mountains from the time he arrived in Berkeley. So, he volunteered for the Tenth Mountain Division, which fought on skis in the Italian campaign. Casualties were enormous. But, in a case of a curse turning into a blessing, he did not become one of those casualties because the army rejected him for poor eyesight (a defect that would later save me, as well). Instead, he spent the war years teaching basic science to undergraduates in an accelerated ROTC program to train them for the army's officers corps.

His lab was in the basement of the UCLA Physics building and it was there, during the war, that he met Evelyn, a striking, tall Jewish woman from Boston who was working as a teaching assistant in physics courses in the same ROTC program. They fell in love, sharing passions for science, the outdoors, politics and folk dancing.

Jacob and Evelyn, December 1945, Los Angeles

She was an extraordinary woman for her generation. Her parents came from Zhitomir in Ukraine and had immigrated to Boston in 1912, part of the greatest mass migration of Jews in history. As opposed to my father's family of origin, where Zionist politics and culture played a central role, they had no ideology and abandoned Jewish religious practice as soon as they reached American shores.

My mother knew nothing of Zionism, an ignorance that would create a significant tension in their marriage. Her parents were uneducated (her mother, Tillie, for whom our daughter Tali is named, never learned to read in any language). Nevertheless, in a kind of educational upward mobility that usually characterized boys among the children of Jewish immigrants, she earned a BA and MA in mathematics and a minor in music (she was a talented pianist). Then, in another sign of independence, she traveled across the United States in 1940 to attend a cousin's wedding in California, but with the intention of staying. She took a job with the Navy in San Diego in a project working on radar, but quit in disgust when they failed to recognize her talent and scientific education, and made her work as a secretary. And thus, she ended up in the basement of the physics building at UCLA.

They married in December 1945 and I was born in July 1949. My father had by now become a very serious scientist, working on the ripening of fruit (especially avocados). But he never lost his passion for Zion. Together with other graduates of youth movements living in Los Angeles – far from their promised land -- he founded Migdal, a socialist Zionist affinity group that met for earnest discussions and celebrated holidays together. This was the alternative, entirely secular "synagogue" in which I grew up.

My father's Zionist dream had been postponed for two decades, but he finally managed to visit the new State of Israel in 1954. He wrote long letters home describing the land he was now discovering first-hand. He was like a kid in a candy store, exploring the length and breadth of the country and delighting in dusting off his slightly archaic Hebrew. He wrote of all the building he witnessed: "I think that the Jews have evidently come here to stay."

That was his wish as well. In 1958, the United Nations sent him there for a year as an agricultural advisor. We landed at the Lod Airport, then a squat building like one finds in airports in the Developing World. People were standing on the roof waving at us as if we had just come home. In some ways I felt I had, perhaps echoing what my father felt tenfold over. We lived in Rehovot, still a somnolent small town, even though the world-renowned Weizmann Institute was there (Chaim Weizmann's personal secretary, whom everyone called Doda (Aunt) Aga, was our upstairs neighbor). When the local public school proved impossible (45 children screaming and I had to do arithmetic exercises on the board in a language I scarcely knew), my father arranged for me and my sister to go to school at Kvutzat Schiller, a kibbutz on the edge of town.

It was the best year of my childhood. I learned to plant a vegetable garden (radishes!), collect eggs from the chicken coop, make an Israeli salad of cucumbers and tomatoes, and speak Hebrew, at least at a 9-year-old level. I joined the Tzofim (the Israeli Scouts) and went on adventures with almost no adult supervision. It was different from my childhood in West Los Angeles in every way possible.

At the end of the year, my father was offered an academic position at the Hebrew University Faculty of Agriculture, located in Rehovot. He wanted to stay, but my mother, embittered by a year in a country she found utterly alien and far too harsh (she refused to learn Hebrew and communicated with the local grocer in Yiddish), insisted on returning to Los Angeles. She won. My father never spoke out loud about his dashed dreams.

In the years that followed, I found it difficult to embrace a typical Jewish childhood in Los Angeles. I made two attempts to attend Hebrew school and either bailed out myself or was ejected by the powers that be. I had my Bar Mitzvah in our backyard and studied Isaiah and Bialik with my father. My main Jewish experience was in the summers when I went to the Brandeis-Bardin sleep-away camp north of Los Angeles. It was there that I discovered for the first time that Judaism could be intellectually exciting as well an intense communal experience. But the year in Israel faded into a distant memory and whatever Hebrew I had learned retreated into the deep recesses of my brain.

When I graduated high school, I went off to Harvard, which had – for reasons inscrutable – accepted me. It was an encounter with what seemed like a foreign, WASP culture, frozen in time. Meanwhile, friends at Berkeley reported the intense excitement of the political counterculture already in full swing. Two visits during the year convinced me that I should try it out. I asked for a year's leave of absence from Harvard. The Freshman Dean, who had to approve the leave, said to me: "You'll come back; they all come back."

I didn't come back. My third day in Berkeley, in Fall 1968, I went walking with new friends from the dorm in the Berkeley Hills. The sky was a crystalline blue. We passed a Berkeley brown shingle house and Vivaldi wafted out of an open window. I knew then that I was here to stay. During that first year in Berkeley, there were demonstrations and riots every quarter, including the infamous People's Park, which I helped build on a gloriously sunny Sunday afternoon. Yet, together with political turmoil, there was real intellectual excitement on the campus. It seemed as if what was going on in the streets and in the classroom were linked together: the material we were studying in courses on political theory, intellectual history and the philosophy of Karl Marx all seemed existentially relevant to the dilemmas of the Vietnam War and racial injustice. I had started Berkeley majoring in chemistry, but soon realized that the real action, at least for me, was not in the laboratory but in the library. Soon enough, I became a history major.

In the summer of 1969, I decided that it was time to visit Israel and to renew the experience I had had had as a nine-year-old. Israel was still in the afterglow of the stunning victory of the 1967 Six Day War. I volunteered at Kibbutz Lahav in the Negev, clearing an abundant crop of rocks from fields (only to have the plow churn up more of them the next day). We got up at 4:00 am and wilted in the summer heat by noon. Life at Lahav was spartan, a taste of an earlier Israel. I found it exhilarating.

I also worked with Bedouin laborers picking apples (although the issue of hired outside labor was hotly contested in the kibbutz movement at the time). They invited me to sleep overnight in their tent, an orientalist experience out of Lawrence of Arabia. After being plied with endless cups of coffee, I asked my host: "Where is the bathroom?" and he replied, with a sweep of his hand: "The whole world is a bathroom!"

Upon returning to Berkeley, I picked up a copy of a free Jewish student newspaper (well, it claimed to cost 10 cents, but nobody I knew ever paid for it) with the promising name of "The Jewish Radical." There I found a long ideological manifesto, "Where We're at and Why?" by a sociology graduate student named Shelly Schreter (later to become one of my closest friends). Shelly wrote:

> The Arab national movement should expect to receive substantial concessions and compensations from the Israelis but they should guard themselves against manifestations of fanatical chauvinism, which so easily degenerate into genocidal racism. Israel, at the same time, should be working toward the goal of enlightened nationalism and should be preparing to take her rightful place as a nation of the Middle East.
>
> And finally, the Jewish radical's personal relationship to the idea of a Jewish national state must be appraised. Entering the evaluation should be the extent of that person's commitment to the struggle for the redemption of America and of his belief in practicalities of ethnically pluralist societies at this point in time.

For some reason, I decided I had to take issue with some of Shelly's argument, contrasting his Zionist Marxism with my own philosophical anarchism. I meant by this position skepticism about nationalism and governments, in favor, instead, of small egalitarian collectives, whether in Israel or America. In truth, I was probably stronger on slogans than I was on substance. I was blown away that the Radical generously agreed to run my piece, even though coming from an outsider. Little did I know then how eager they were for submissions by almost anyone who could type something at least semi-coherent. And, so, with equal measures of passion and chutzpah, I wrote:

I agree that it is now time to work within the Jewish community to emphasize our radical criticism of modern society. Let us gather together amongst those Jews who have the self-confidence of which I speak and create living and cultural groups to serve as examples for those we cannot move with our words.

In my view Israel could profit well by immigration of serious, dedicated American youth who bring both radical social ideas as well as a commitment to Judaism. What we must do now, whether we have in mind Aliyah or not, is to unite those self-confident Jewish individuals in a new youth movement patterned after the great Zionist youth movements of Europe of half a century ago, yet with our own modern viewpoint and historical commitment.

Once I met the members of the group, I realized that these were my kindred spirits, or, as we called it then, my *hevre* (an untranslatable Hebrew term meaning both friends and comrades). Without be aware of it, I was soon to relive my father's experience in the youth movement in Poland.

However, whatever involvement the group – the Radical Jewish Union (RJU) – might have had in store for me would soon have to be put aside until the following academic year. By early 1970, I had decided that I needed to return to Israel for a longer stint that would include the spring quarter and the following summer. I was subject to the American draft, so I had to arrange phony credits with a sympathetic professor in order to maintain my student status (he was very surprised later on that I actually did all the reading he had assigned me). I arrived in April 1970, just in time to join the annual March to Jerusalem, a patriotic event organized by the army that included a cross-section of Israeli society; following the Six Day War, the march took place in the West Bank. We walked through villages north of Jerusalem. The local Palestinians weren't overtly hostile, but the realization suddenly struck me: they don't want us here. That was the moment I woke up to the impossibility of the Occupation.

I spent the spring back at Kibbutz Lahav, nearly burning down the kibbutz while incinerating chickens that had died of Newcastle disease. Then, in July, I started Hebrew classes at the Ulpan Akiva in Netanya for the rest of the summer. My Hebrew had begun to resurrect itself the previous summer and I became obsessed with improving it. I listened to records of Israeli songs and translated them. I insisted on speaking Hebrew to everyone in Israel. So, when I got to the ulpan, they put me in the highest class, which was only scheduled for the month of July. I would be free and with no plans for the month of August.

Nothing could have been more fortuitous. One of the other students, with whom I became friendly, Navah Haber-Schaim, had come to the ulpan from Boston before enlisting in the Israeli army. The kibbutz and the Korati family would be Navah's home-away-from-home while in the army. I had actually heard of the kibbutz, which was on the border with Jordan, because the previous spring, they were featured in the newspaper, having been shelled by the PLO on the night of Passover. They had moved the Passover seder into a bomb shelter and celebrated the holiday there. Looking back on it now, I suppose I was young, full of testosterone, and naively attracted to seeing the "action" up close on a border kibbutz. I asked Navah if I might tag along.

I had already met several members of the Korati clan. When Navah and I spent a Shabbat in Jerusalem during the ulpan, we ran into Racheli's brother Gil and his wife Debbie by sheer coincidence in a falafel joint on Ben Yehuda St. And later on, after Navah had inquired about my coming to the kibbutz as a volunteer, Racheli's mother, Anina, stopped by the ulpan to meet me. Wise woman that she was, she was probably already checking me out to see if I'd pass muster to join the family. Did I have expectations about meeting Racheli? I can't reconstruct them, but I certainly learned from Navah that she was someone special, with interests not far from mine.

So, there I was, awkwardly entering the wrong door. As I remember, Navah was already there, as was Anina. I was given a cold drink (much needed!) and cake. And then the door opened and, without exaggeration, a force of nature, the likes of which I had never met, blew into the room. She had very short, dark brown hair (a subject of much further discussion), wore wooden clogs and a sleeveless shirt. She was both very intense and very funny. I don't remember what we talked about, but she talked a mile-a-minute. As a result of the year her family had spent in Boston, not only was her English excellent but she had also tasted the American counter-culture. We went back and forth from English to Hebrew.

In short order, I discovered that she was asking many of the same questions as I was about Judaism, Jewish philosophy and Jewish identity. She was nine days shy of her eighteenth birthday the day we met, but I sensed an intellectual and emotional maturity I had never before encountered. For the next nearly four weeks, we discussed Franz Rosenzweig, A.D. Gordon, Martin Buber, the Bible and who knows what else? We claimed to disagree with each other about everything, but that was a foolish pose. We would meet for breakfast and lunch, when she was supposed to be studying for her matriculation exams and I was supposed to be assembling irrigation pipes in 100-degree weather. The breakfasts and lunches lasted longer and longer.

It wasn't all serious talk. We sang songs from the Beatles and from *Hair*, sharing a common cultural language. We horsed around, cracking jokes and making fun of each other. If we had been a little more self-aware, we would have realized that all this was flirtation. I became the butt of ridicule when I ran for the bomb shelter through a trench during a night-time shelling dressed only in my underwear. We went folk dancing -- I had become something of a fanatical folk dancer in Berkeley -- only to discover that Racheli couldn't dance at all. We had a good laugh about my work partner, a strange Australian named Raymond who complained that the Israeli government should have been consulting with him about the low-intensity conflict in the Jordan Valley because he "knew people in high places." After I left the kibbutz, Raymond ended up in a psychiatric hospital.

The heat in the Beit She'an Valley that summer was oppressive. I was housed in a wooden "Swedish hut" (a prefab imported from Scandinavia in the early years of the kibbutz). Wooden structures like this heated up even more than the more-recent concrete houses and only kibbutz members had air conditioning. The first night, the weak fan that came with my room barely cut the heat and I got very little sleep. The second night, I had a bright idea: sleep in one of the bomb shelters that dotted the kibbutz landscape. It certainly was cooler down there, but just as I started to get to sleep, a parade of older kibbutz members came in and made quite a racket. They were down there not to escape the heat but to escape the PLO shellings. And, as (bad) luck would have it, such a shelling took place my third night, when Racheli instructed us to shelter under the bed in her parents' apartment. Well, I didn't get any sleep that night either, especially when another random shell landed with a bang at 2:00 or 3:00 in the morning.

And, yet, no overt romance that month, or, at least, none that we would admit to each other at the time. We were both very young and inexperienced: neither of us had had a serious relationship. Besides, we were also overly cerebral and, despite our garrulousness, rather inhibited. And, so, as Racheli has already written, what developed would take a long time and hundreds of letters.

Prologue 3: Racheli

GROWING UP BELOW SEA LEVEL

IT TOOK MANY TWISTS and turns and a couple of narrow escapes from incoming shells and grenades for David not only to arrive at my kibbutz and quickly lodge himself in my parents' apartment, but then to slowly and gradually, sink roots into my life. But to arrive at that moment, we need to go back many years, long before I was born. My parents, Anina Vohryzek and Kurt Tramer (later Anina and Chaim Korati) were both born in Czechoslovakia, my mother in Prague and my father in Ostrava. My mother was the first child, followed four years later by a brother (Josef, aka Pepik) of an upwardly mobile middle-class Jewish family. Her mother was one of eight children born in a small town in Bohemia. The family's point of pride was her grandfather's position in the local police force. Maria, my mother's mother, had grander aspirations and moved to Prague as a young woman. There she met Jakob, a self-made young lawyer who had lost his own parents and left his uncle's home at age fourteen when he was about to be sent to a yeshiva to become a rabbi. He, too, came to Prague, as my mother liked to say "without a penny in his pocket," found work and put himself through law school. As a young couple in Prague, Maria and Jakob entered the cultural and intellectual world of Jews who were highly integrated into European society and Czech language and culture, befriending luminaries such as Max Brod. Jakob and Maria managed to get both of their children out of Prague after the Nazi invasion in 1939: my mother to Palestine and her brother, then only fourteen years old, to Sweden. Their repeated efforts to get exit visas for themselves all came to naught and they were both murdered by the Nazis.

My father's trajectory was, in some ways, similar. His Ostrava family owned small businesses, the most important one was his grandfather's butcher shop which was split down the middle between a kosher side serving the Jewish community and a *treif* one selling pork to the Gentiles. His father, Josef, was a dreamer – like his biblical namesake and his surname, Tramer (Träumer in German) -- but his dreams focused on wealth and the good life, more than on cultural and intellectual accomplishments. Josef, too, set out for Prague as a young man. There he met and married Berta, who came from a petite-bourgeois family that owned a shop of dry goods in Prague's Jewish Quarter.

It was Josef's first marriage and probably the only one based on any kind of romance. He divorced Berta when my father was a very young boy and went on to marry six other women, each a wealthy, aging widow. After running through each wife's assets to support his *bon vivant* life style, he would graciously agree to a divorce with no strings attached, and go on to the next widow. As a result, my father was raised by his mother and her two sisters and brother, all living in the same household. Occasionally, his father would visit him, sometimes taking him to a lavish meal in a fancy restaurant (on the upswing with one of his widows) at other times, with barely enough coins in his pocket to buy him an ice cream. My father's two aunts and uncle, as well as his father, managed to get out Europe in time to escape the Nazis.

But not Berta. She was deported to Terezin in 1942 and then to Auschwitz, where she was murdered. Many years later, I saw a postcard that she sent from Auschwitz saying that she was healthy. Later still, David deduced from his historical research that Berta was part of the so-called "Czech Family Camp" in Auschwitz, two groups of 5,000 Jews each sent from Terezin to Auschwitz to dupe the Red Cross into thinking that Auschwitz was a benign labor camp. When the Red Cross declined to visit Auschwitz, they were all sent to the gas chambers.

My mother imbibed Maria and Jakob's values of humanism, universalism and staunch independence of mind. My father's main legacy from his childhood was a fierce self-reliance and a rather cynical view of most of humanity. And, like David's father, the formative experience of my parents' adolescence was in the Zionist youth movement, in their case, Maccabi Hatzair (politically more moderate than Jacob Biale's Hashomer Hatzair, but also dedicated to living on a kibbutz). There, they learned about Zionism, embraced a longing for Eretz Israel, became committed to idealistic dreams about kibbutz life, and were fortunate enough to get a life-line out of Europe in 1940.

The Nazis had occupied Czechoslovakia in March 1939. To reach Eretz Israel, the land of their dreams, required negotiating exit visas from the Nazis. My father actually had an interview with Adolf Eichmann, the notorious Gestapo official in charge of Jewish emigration. Eichmann asked my father what his occupation was and what work he planned to pursue in Palestine. "A farmer," my father said. "Show me your hands," Eichmann ordered. He looked at my father's hands: "You're no farmer," he said, but then muttered "your problem," and still gave him a visa. Not that much of a surprise since Eichmann's goal at that point was forcing as many Jews as possible to leave Europe. A few years later, he organized the deportations of Jews throughout. Europe to the death camps.

My parents, Summer 1939

On December 10, 1939, my parents left their homes and families in Prague. There were numerous points along their perilous journey when their trajectory could have been thwarted. A planned short sojourn in Bratislava the day after they left Prague's Masaryk Train Station turned into eight months of incarceration while the Danube froze for the winter months and in spring one bureaucratic hurdle after another popped up. Finally, they set sail down the Danube in August 1940 and arrived at the Black Sea port of Tulcea, in Romania. More delays, fees required and, certainly, some bribes; a month later they boarded a retrofitted cargo ship to sail to Palestine. Their ship, the *Atlantic*, was one of three that launched the same day, each holding roughly 1,600 Jewish refugees. They came from Prague, Vienna and Danzig. A handful were prisoners released from Dachau, from whom they heard first-hand about the horrors of the concentration camps.

Once in the Mediterranean, the *Atlantic* quickly ran low on food, water and coal. On October 28, three weeks into the voyage, the *Atlantic's* crew of Greek sailors of dubious repute heard on the radio that Italy had invaded Greece. Fearful about transporting "enemy Jews" while flying a Panamanian flag, they abandoned the ship at night, but not before dumping nearly all its remaining coal overboard. The passengers took control of the ship. They broke down most of the ship's wooden parts and fed them to the furnace, including a piano from the once-more-glamorous dining deck. But two days later there was nothing left to burn and they consigned their fate to the prevailing winds of the Mediterranean.

After several days of drifting on the sea's waves the passengers woke up to a miracle: land on the horizon! Following nail-biting, seemingly endless minutes tracking a speedboat heading their way, they identified the Union Jack. The deck erupted in *God Save The King*. But it was Cyprus they had reached, not Palestine. A few weeks later, the Royal Navy escorted the *Atlantic* to the Haifa Harbor, where the passengers now sang their own national anthem, *Hatikvah*. But joy soon turned to doom, as they were informed that they would be loaded onto the triple-deck *Patria* (if I had made this name up as an artistic device, you'd think it was pure kitsch), anchored about one hundred yards from the dock.

When the first *Atlantic* passengers embarked onto the *Patria's* deck late in the evening of November 24 and in the early morning of the 25, they quickly learned it was much worse than even their most pessimistic nightmares: *all of them*, along with the 2,500 who had set out with them from Tulcea on the two other boats and had arrived two weeks earlier, were being deported to Mauritius, a remote tropical island in the Indian Ocean, under British rule.

At 9:14 AM on November 25, as my parents were about to step into the launch that ferried *Atlantic* passengers to the *Patria* in groups of forty, there was a deafening explosion. The *Patria* flipped onto its side and began sinking in the harbor. Most of its passengers were rescued in the course of the day, but over 250 (including about 50 British soldiers and policemen) drowned. Everyone was transferred to the detention camp in Atlit, about 12 miles south of Haifa. Ten days later those who had survived the *Patria* explosion were permitted to remain in Palestine as a humanitarian gesture, while the 1,580 passengers still on the *Atlantic,* my parents included, were deported to Mauritius a few days later.

They arrived in Port Louis on Christmas Day, 1940 and were imprisoned there. In the spring of 1942, my father was able to join several dozen young men who volunteered to serve in the British Army's "Free Czech Army" unit. They travelled to Alexandria, Egypt, ready to fight the advancing German army. But the Germans were defeated at El Alamein and my father was spared actual battle. He was then posted to Palestine as a British soldier. In August 1945, after the war had ended, my mother and the rest of the Mauritius detainees finally arrived in Palestine, permitted to enter legally.

My parents met and fell in love on the spot. They had known each other, of course, since their early teens in the youth movement in Prague, but all those years they had been *haverim* – friends and comrades -- not romantic partners. From September 1945 to July 1946, they mostly wrote each other between my father's limited time off as a soldier and my mother's grueling schedule as a nurse's aide. They had only about a half a dozen actual dates. They exchanged more than one hundred letters over eleven months – a remarkable foreshadowing of the love letters between David and me on which this book is based. Written in English in order to pass the British military censor, they also make for compelling reading today as a window into that moment in history.

My father was demobilized in July 1946 and, soon after, they arrived, at long last, at Kibbutz Kfar Ruppin, joining their youth movement comrades who had arrived earlier. As they anticipated going to Kfar Ruppin in their letters, they discussed buying a fan, the kind of small table-top fan David reports did little good in 1970. But it was too expensive: about 6.5 Pounds Sterling. That sum - about

$350 in today's currency – was insurmountable on the salary of a soldier or a nurse's aide at the Afula hospital (where my two brothers and I would be born). So, it was without a fan that they arrived at the place of their dreams, welcomed by their comrades and the stultifying summer heat.

Anina and Chaim, Kfar Ruppin, 1946

It was that same heat that marked my childhood. But, as a young child, you don't know better: it seemed perfectly reasonable to spend hot afternoons lying on the tile floor in the kindergarten room, after the *metapelet* (caretaker) had thrown down a bucket of water to cool us off a little more. The question of how my parents, who had grown up in temperate Prague, tolerated it, never entered my mind. But I did grow up sensing, without explicit words, how much they longed for what their childhood offered: the beautiful streets of Prague's

Old Town, winter skiing, soft summer dusks lingering for hours, and warm summer days picking mushrooms and berries in cool, dark forests. I somehow longed for those things too. More than anything else, I pined for the real forest, the kind you read about in fairy tales. At age fifteen, I first set foot in a European forest when we visited Switzerland en route to the United States. I was swept up by a profound feeling: *THIS is the forest I have been dreaming of all my life!*

I was raised in a kibbutz Children's House, which meant that I spent all day there (before I reached school age), would go to my parents' apartment from about 4:00 to 8:00 pm and then would sleep with my classmates. We were left alone during part of our afternoon naptime and in the evenings before the night caretaker arrived. That led to all manner of wild antics, but, fortunately, without any injuries. Along with the giddy freedom came a huge weight of responsibility for each other. When one boy in my kindergarten room would occasionally wet his bed, the three of us who shared the room would wake up at dawn, change his sheets and get him clean pajamas. To this day I don't know if either our metapelet or this boy's parents actually knew that he still wet his bed.

———————

The trajectory from those early dawns and nightly episodes of mischief to the young woman David met in summer 1970 was typical for a kibbutz girl in the 1950's and early 60's: a very close-knit class of eleven kids living, studying and working together. Work was the pinnacle of our day: at first in the children's farm where we grew vegetables and tended chickens, ducks, goats and sheep and, after third grade, "graduating" to working in the real branches of the kibbutz. After work, we had a couple of hours of play with no adult supervision. Soccer was king, and I was the only girl on the team, until my breasts started showing.

Despite the few hours I spent with my parents each day, their influence was paramount. I imbibed their nonconformism, their very broad cultural horizons (their library of mostly English books covered a whole wall of their apartment), their humanism and kibbutz idealism. The latter was tempered by a rather sober, if not outright cynical, view of people's foibles and pettiness, including those of their fellow kibbutz members.

It was the broad cultural horizons, in literature, philosophy, art and music that, in a way, prepared me for a year in Boston in 1967-68, a year that challenged and eventually upended my "kibbutznik-for-life" expectations. By coincidence, 1967-68 was the same year that David spent at Harvard; we were across the Charles River from each other, but never met. It was in a way a parallel, formative experience to David's year in Israel in 1958-59. While David's father was sent by the UN to Israel, my father was sent by UNESCO to the US to work on physics teaching methods with Navah's father, Uri Haber-Schaim. His group of physicists pioneered innovative, hands-on ways of teaching science. My father had initiated a similar approach to teaching physics completely on his own. With only a high school diploma plus a few physics courses at the Hebrew University in 1960 (the kibbutz had sent him to take as many courses as he could of the three-year BA degree in just one year) he became the physics teacher at our local high school.

So, a mere three weeks after the Six-Day-War, my family boarded a plane for Switzerland, on our way to the US. My eldest brother, Gil, was already serving in the IDF, so he had to stay back. My brother Eran had just graduated high school and was looking forward to a year of thrilling freedom and adventure, having been able to postpone his draft. The apex of his year was joining the student revolution in France in May 1968. He met us in late June, as we began our trip back home through Europe, with all buttons of his shirt blown off when a gendarme chased him in the streets of Paris and grabbed him by the collar.

My year was more structured: I attended Newton High School. I didn't have any buttons blown off, but it certainly did, as they said then, "blow my mind." Newton High School (North), at the time widely-considered "the best public high school in America," was rife with student activism. I was very intrigued and hitched my wagon to a group of students who were working on housing discrimination and other racial justice issues, and opposition to the Vietnam War. I was moved by their idealism but, at first, felt there was no connection or parallel to life in Israel, where there were no Blacks and no "unjust war."

However, almost imperceptibly, the scales of conventional opinions fell from my eyes. We had no Blacks in Israel, but we did have Arabs, and Sephardi and Mizrahi Jews, each discriminated against in political, social and cultural ways. The Six-Day-War was justified for Israel's survival, but the continued occupation of the West Bank and Gaza. . . was that necessary? And just? The seeds of doubt were sown, although it took returning home to acknowledge them. Perhaps more than the specific issues, what really blew open my horizons was the example of the students I met who did not believe their government, neither its claims about "liberty and justice for all," nor its pronouncements about the war.

I also discovered a form of Jewishness that I had never encountered before. It began with a surprise. In early October, after I had attended a couple of meetings, the boy who had brought me into the group and sported the ubiquitous crewcut and penny loafers, told me there was no meeting that week because it was Rosh Hashanah.

"You know what Rosh Hashanah is?" I asked, utterly floored.

"Of course!" he said.

"You are Jewish?" I still couldn't digest the information.

"Of course," he said, "pretty much everyone in the group is. Except the two Black guys."

A window was suddenly thrown open for me, seeing a deeply-held Jewish identity that was neither Israeli nor Israel-centered. It was a first stepping stone in my exploration of Jewishness, which was to preoccupy David and me in the summer of 1970.

Shortly before returning to Israel, I had a vivid dream that really disturbed me. In the dream, I am back at the Children's House at my kibbutz, surrounded by my classmates. I open my suitcase and take out the presents I brought for my class: a record player for which I had saved my baby-sitting money all year long and some Beatles records, the *Hair* album, and Mozart's *Eine Kleine Nachtmusik* (trying to educate my classmates, I guess...). I actually did bring these gifts, but in the dream, my classmates grab the record player and try to operate it, doing it all wrong, as I keep protesting "That's not the way *we* do it in America."

The record player was a huge hit with my classmates, but within a couple of months of my return it became evident that "you can't keep them down on the farm once they have seen Paris." I was out of sync with my peers, both in world outlook and in schoolwork. In key subjects my year in the US had catapulted me way ahead of my class. I was restless and began to pester the teachers with impossible questions. I imagine I exuded an intolerable sense of superiority since *I had been to America*. I found the company of my classmates simply boring while, I am sure, they found my stories of men with long hair, critiques of societal discrimination, and questioning your own government weird, if not obnoxious.

In November 1968, overcoming the resistance of our local school, I transferred to Beit Yerach, the Jordan Valley Regional High School, on the banks of the Sea of Galilee. Beit Yerach was a much larger and more academically rigorous high school. All subjects were taught at a much higher level than I had been used to, but it was Jewish Studies that had a formative impact on me. The teacher, Ehud Luz (son of Kadish Luz, the revered first speaker of Israel's Knesset), who went by the nickname Uda (all kibbutz schools were very informal and teachers were always addressed by first names or nicknames) threw open an intellectual doorway to Jewish history and thought, from rabbinic texts to modern Jewish philosophy.

And the perspectives I brought with me from the year in

America found a more receptive audience. Together with my best friend, Devorale Veiner, I chose for my senior-year project to create an illustrated history of the Beatles. It was well received by my classmates, who were all Beatles fans and by my teachers as well, who acknowledged it was a significant topic. Only five years earlier, the Israeli government had banned a proposed concert by the Beatles on the grounds that it was "of no artistic value." I also wrote a senior thesis about the portrayal of Arabs in Israeli literature, another manifestation of my political awakening.

As a natural continuation of our philosophical discussions, I introduced David to Uda by taking him to a meeting of a small study group at Uda's house in Kibbutz Degania Bet. We met once a week and studied Jewish thinkers like A.D. Gordon, Martin Buber and Franz Rosenzweig. It was thanks to this study group that I could hold my own in conversations with a college senior from UC Berkeley. And it was a moment of triumph for me to bring him with me and impress him with Uda's teaching and with the level of the discussion.

Uda conveyed very clearly his respect for us as his students, as I recounted in a letter to David in October 1970, after taking one of the matriculation exams. I was scandalized by the amount of cheating and observed that nothing of this sort had happened at Beit Yerach.

> *No one in my class would ever think of cheating on Uda's tests, and he knew it – and thus, usually left for most of the time while we were taking a test to do other things. Why cheat with Uda when you can ask him anything you don't remember – and he'll tell you?"*

The night after the study session with Uda became the second chapter in that month's "adventures with beds." We stayed overnight in Kibbutz Degania Aleph. Navah had come along, as she too wanted to meet my cherished teacher. It was a small room, perhaps 10 ft by 12ft, with two narrow metal beds pushed against opposite walls and a mattress on the floor between them taking up every inch of space between the two beds. Perhaps what I am remembering is not so much the physical mattress as my guilt about poor Navah, stuck in the middle between David and me, as we continued discussing Jewish philosophy into the wee hours.

David took off the next morning to visit his relatives in Kibbutz Mishmar Ha-Emek and then we met up a few days later in Jerusalem. The night before David and I were to part, we stayed at the apartment of Danny Bahat, a prominent Israeli archeologist and family friend. We sat and talked for hours, this time without any beds involved but, rather, on a stone wall outside the apartment. In my fuzzy, romantic memory, we talked until we glimpsed the faint light of dawn. But maybe I already sensed that it was our relationship that was dawning.

The next day we said goodbye at the Rockefeller Museum. He went off to America, back to Berkeley, while I was poised to take my very first steps into adulthood. I didn't know how to define what had happened between us or what to call it. But I knew enough not to let it be dissipated by distance and completely divergent life trajectories.

At the Rockefeller Museum (not our lamb's skin coat)

Chapter 1

AN INTELLECTUAL FLIRTATION
September -- December 1970

THURSDAY, SEPTEMBER 10, 1970: RACHELI

My first letter was newsy and chatty, written as if to preserve the three-way friendship between me, David and Navah. Did I know better somewhere in the depths of my heart? Does the fact that I wrote it at 1:00 am tell us that there was more to it? In the Song of Songs, the female lover says: "I am asleep, but my heart is awake. The sound of my lover knocking ..."

Dear David,

It's 1 AM a.m. now, do you know where your children are?

This was a much-too-often-repeated joke between us (we'll save you the annoyance by not reproducing it every time it appears in our letters), referring to the way the late evening news concluded every night during the year I spent in Newton (an upscale neighborhood of Boston). As I recall, it was Walter Cronkite, signing off, but a quick check tells me he wasn't on that late and his signature closing was

"And that's the way it is," followed by the date of the broadcast. That is a false memory, since it was actually the closing of the late-night news in Boston. Remembering it that way probably reflects how much Cronkite's reporting of the Martin Luther King and Robert Kennedy assassinations left its stamp on my experience of the year in America.

I conveyed dramatic news from the day of David's departure: another near-miss with explosives, of which he was not aware at the time:

One thing I know you <u>missed</u> is a hand grenade that exploded in the street in front of the Flower Gate of the Old City of Jerusalem, 3 - 5 minutes after <u>you</u> were there. . . By the way, no one was seriously hurt.

In keeping with our summer conversations, I turned immediately to philosophical questions. And, yet, at the same time, without saying so explicitly, I was already indicating how much I missed him.

We had a good chug [study group] on Sunday – well it was good because Uda talked mostly about Buber. But this time it did lack something because there was no serious discussion – I only made a few comments and arguments but it didn't develop into a full discussion. You had to have been there! The point is one of the things I like most about Buber is his anarchism [Martin Buber thought that each person could find an immediate relationship to God without the commandments]. It seems to me the only possible approach I could take to Judaism.

But I may be wrong– sometimes I think that Franz Rosenzweig's approach [that one could make a personal commitment to perform some of the commandments] seems impossible for me because I really don't have a strong enough willpower. It's sort of nice to escape into speculations and to seek your Jewish identity – it is romantic (like in the books - you <u>have to</u> read Madame Bovary!)

And so on, and on and on, until I conclude: "Since I'm finishing the page and it is 2:00 am... and I get up at 6 AM – I must end the letter. WRITE!" And write he did!

SEPTEMBER 13, 1970: DAVID

I did not, of course, know that Racheli had written me three days before, so I imagined that I was launching our correspondence. That we scarcely said goodbye when we parted at the Rockefeller Museum was no doubt a reflection of how much remained unsaid between us.

The nonchalant nature of the goodbyes we exchanged was fitting and proper to my mood, at least. It was as if we were parting for a day or two. I shall now definitely have to return to say goodbye properly.

Read fifty years later, it is evident that I was already conveying something much more serious than a flippant gesture, but whether I knew it then, I can hardly say.

I had walked from the Rockefeller Museum past the Flowers Gate to the Old City of Jerusalem, unaware that I had just missed becoming the target of a grenade, to go to the bus station and from there to the airport. By the evening, I was in London. I spent a day and half there, saw a theatrical production of the Canterbury Tales and was jolted awake by a loud noise outside my hotel window that, at first, I thought was a PLO shell. It was probably a car backfiring. While awaiting my charter flight home, I drank too much beer in a pub, vomited for the first and only time from too much alcohol, and then slept the whole way home.

In that first letter, I reported on what it was like to be back home in a poor-man's imitation of Allen Ginsberg:

How do I find Los Angeles after all these months? The essence of bourgeois plastic Jesus, neon-lit smog in the eye, crowded freeway, hole in the flag (don't put it down), long-haired, short-sighted, big mouthed, Coke-swilling, Bible-quoting, guitar-plucking, radical Jew Commie, John Birch Society member walking his poodle in Disneyland quoting Marx, Mao and the Constitution in five-part harmony. In short and in brief: HOME.

Perhaps the inspiration for this incoherent rant was a concert I had attended the night before in the Hollywood Bowl with Pete Seeger, Joan Baez and Arlo Guthrie playing the music of Woody Guthrie. I wrote of my reaction to this music: "Yes, Virginia, America does have culture. There is something so evocatively American about Guthrie's folk songs that makes you realize how American you are – a good, but disturbing welcome home." I signed off saying that I had to go "give a talk to a group of Jews about LIFE IN A BORDER SETTLEMENT IN ISRAEL. It shall be very brief, as befits my knowledge."

Did I have even a faint inkling that this was my first contribution to what would mushroom to 258 letters? Of course not. But there was something in the spirit of this letter that carried over from the month at Kfar Ruppin and that promised more than just occasional news bulletins.

SEPTEMBER 18, 1970: DAVID

Since Racheli had written first, I soon had a letter to answer, which I did in Hebrew:

You know that you now have to do some "Zionist work," namely, to write to me a lot so my connection to Israel will remain strong and so I'll be convinced to come there next year. If you do that, I will collect all your letters and when I am old and famous, I'll show them to the whole world and say: these were written by the kibbutznik who convinced me to make Aliyah to Israel.

And where will this kibbutznik be, or, more precisely, will she know where the children are? That is the question!

The answer to that question would be many years coming and would not end up either on kibbutz or in Israel. But already in response to the question "do you know where your children are?" there was a hint that this correspondence might, in the end, provide an answer.

SEPTEMBER 19, 1970: DAVID

While I was still in Los Angeles, I went to hear a sermon by Rabbi Harold Schulweis who had greatly impressed me the previous year. Schulweis combined a powerful intellect and deep Jewish knowledge with an equally profound spiritual sensibility. He was one of my earliest teachers of Judaica. I found his lecture on the Hasidic tale so inspiring that I had to describe it to Racheli immediately, even though I had just written to her the day before.

> *The Hasidic tale humanizes God and divinizes man by taking the mundane and profane and deriving from it a lesson. For the Hasidim there is no separation between the sacred and the ordinary worlds; everything in the world contains a divine spark and therefore the most base and trivial thing contains a tie to God. A mitnaged [opponent of Hasidism] once asked a Hasid why he goes so often to see the tsaddik. The Hasid replied that he goes to watch him lace and unlace his shoes.*

> *I have a lot of other ideas on the role of the Hasidic tale. But instead of writing them here, I will send you a paper I wrote on Elie Wiesel (since you have finally woken to his greatness) ... It is amazing how a lot of things we discussed during the summer pop up in the paper, though a lot more coherent than my usual mumblings.*

I have since long cooled to Elie Wiesel, whom I had met two years earlier, but in those years, his novelistic reworkings of Hasidic tales exerted a profound influence on both me and Racheli.

In response to Racheli's report on the discussion of Buber vs. Rosenzweig in her Judaism study group, I wrote tongue-in-cheek:

> *I'm glad to hear that you are in full swing in pursuit of your Jewish identity (in spite of imminent failure on the bagrut [matriculation exams]). Very romantic indeed. I picture it as a movie with Paul Newman, an earnest young Jew in search of his identity personified seductively by Julie Christie – do not be misled by her last name. Riding over rugged mountains, crossing raging rivers, fighting off evil anti-Semites disguised as Mexican bandits, he achieves his goal but dies at the last minute of an overdose of chicken soup (the title of this epic might be "Hombrele" or "Cool Hand Moshe").*

As to her urging that I read *Madame Bovary*, I appended a postscript that I had already started the novel: "hurrah for books!"

SEPTEMBER 22, 1970: RACHELI

I waited to get a letter from David before writing again. I suspect I was nervous: would he write to me as quickly as I wished? Would the letters flow as naturally as our conversations had? Would we be able to be ourselves through the written word (even though those selves were partly a pose each one of us adopted to appear smart, but without being too open and, thus, vulnerable)? I was greatly relieved to get David's first letter about eight days after I had written mine. I said, when replying, "I was glad to get your cheerful letter – especially because it is <u>so you</u>."

I wrote my second letter in the hopes it would land in David's mailbox right on the Eve of Rosh Hashanah (September 30 that year). I fashioned a somewhat corny calligraphy of "Shanah Tovah" with the first letter of each word depicted as a dove. Corny or not, peace was very much on my mind: "as we approach the start of 5731 the situation here is very grave, given the tragedy in Jordan. Very peaceful in Kfar Ruppin since trouble started in Jordan but we can hear the booms from there." I was referring to "Black September," King Hussein of Jordan's wholesale attack on the PLO and other Palestinian militias (called *Fadayeen*) which resulted in thousands of Palestinians killed and thousands more, including the leadership, exiled to Lebanon and Syria. The bombings that had sent us under the bed abruptly ended as a result of the fighting in Jordan. The irony of peace, or at least, quiet in Kfar Ruppin, thanks to war in Jordan clearly troubled me. Hardly anyone in Israel viewed the decimation of the PLO in Jordan as a "tragedy." I wonder, in hindsight, how I came to that view. Was it a premonition, though not worked out in any detail, that this was just one chapter of the Israeli-Palestinian conflict? Less than two years later, the Black September terrorist group carried out the massacre of eleven Israeli athletes at the Munich Olympics.

Israel's leaders were more optimistic. Israeli Defense Minister Moshe Dayan's Rosh Hashanah radio interview gave a rather upbeat assessment of Israel's political and security situation:

He made two important points: he sees the end of war, fighting – not peace but the end of the 3.5-year continued war [referring the War of Attrition after the 1967 War]. With Nasser dead, we'll have a longer cease fire on the Suez Canal, even if not formally declared. Second -- if there is no strong leadership in Egypt, the Russians will have more influence. And the Russians don't want a war with Israel and they can't afford one.

Gamal Abdel Nassar had ruled Egypt with an iron fist from 1952 to 1970, led Egypt through wars with Israel (the Sinai Campaign in '56 and the Six Day War in '67) and died of a heart attack in September 1970. But Dayan's optimism proved to be short-lived: unbeknownst to us, the three years of relative quiet would end with the devastating Yom Kippur War in October 1972.

Dayan was also optimistic about the Palestinians:

He sees a very positive change of attitude among the Arabs in the Occupied Territories. They cooperate with the administration and most important – there has never (since the war) been so little co-operation with the terrorists as there is now. So – this is good news for the start of 5731.

He was as wrong about the Palestinians as about the Egyptians: the Palestinians would later resist Israeli rule with two fierce uprisings.

OCTOBER 2, 1970: DAVID

A few days after my September 19 letter, I traveled from Los Angeles to Berkeley to start my senior year. I was happy to be back. I took two friends from out of town around campus and wrote: "I really wish you could be here because it is very beautiful. The trees, grass, streams – it's no wonder that nobody gets any studying done." I was also happy to get Racheli's New Year's letter with its pacifist sentiments: "I suppose that New Year's is the time we should put aside all our usual cynicism and try to see far enough into the future when maybe our sons will not have the sword hanging over their heads as it does over ours." Our correspondence was already becoming pregnant with meaning: "'Two of us writing letters ... on our way back home.' So, Berkeley becomes Kfar Ruppin, Kfar Ruppin becomes Berkeley ... almost. Thank God for the Beatles."

With two roommates, I had moved into an apartment on Durant Avenue above Top Dog, a popular hot dog joint, still there today (living above it was enough to lessen the attraction). But directly below my window was a ramp for wheelchairs into a small apartment labeled "Center for Independent Living." Little did I know that the people going up and down that ramp were the first activists of the disability rights movement; one of whom, Jim LeBrecht, is now our very dear friend.

One of my roommates kept kosher. He gave me a book to read about it, evidently hoping to win a convert. I wrote to Racheli:

I've done a lot of thinking about it, but I don't believe that it would be at all meaningful to me. I somehow believe I could be a Jew without that. It's like the discussions we had about Rosenzweig: how can you be religious because of an abstract, intellectual decision to do so? Either you are brought up that way or it is very artificial to pretend that you are religious. I don't believe that the motions themselves are meaningful.

Enough philosophizing: I had to end because a number of us were heading down to the Monterey Folk Festival to hear Joan Baez, Mimi Farina and other icons of the 60s.

OCTOBER 2, 1970: RACHELI

I had received David's paper about Elie Wiesel and the challenge of Jewish atheism. Ellen, the nosy secretary of the kibbutz who distributed the members' letters every day, wanted to know who, and what, and why is sending me manuscripts through the mail. I was duly impressed by the paper, but perhaps more impressive was the way we were struggling over the same questions:

Why did you underline this? "The easy path through atheism does not lead to truth because it is a denial of the struggle, a choosing of apathy over commitment." Do you think so? This is where I disagree -- atheism is not a __denial__ – certainly not a denial of the past. I was thinking this on Erev Rosh Hashanah – about leading a traditional Jewish life -- to a certain extent as an atheist. I had to write it down and later I read your essay and found it in there (of course, better said). It's amazing!

My thoughts sounded remarkably similar to what David would write a few days later (the letters had crossed somewhere over the Atlantic Ocean):

Suddenly I understood that it's not necessary to believe in God in order to be Jewish. You have to believe: believe in Am Yisrael [the People of Israel], in belonging to it, to its history. You have to believe that you, as an individual, have a role to play in this world.

I went on and on about finding your place and your role in the continuity of Jewish history from one generation to the next. But then I feel compelled to poke some holes in my hot air balloon: "But, it's hard for me to believe whole-heartedly; in such a cynical world, inevitably you sometimes look at yourself from the outside -- and see that you are ridiculous."

I replied in detail to David's description of Schulweis' sermon about the Hasidic story:

A day before I got your letter, we had a meeting with Uda in which he talked about -- guess what? – the Hasidic concept of "sanctify yourself through that which is permitted" [a Talmudic saying], as the attempt to expand the boundaries of Halakhah [Jewish law] and the mitzvot [commandments] to cover areas of life that are neutral (i.e. not regulated by law), seeing Judaism as a totalizing concept. Rosenzweig and Buber, as well as Gordon (in his view of life) are close to this Hasidic idea [A.D. Gordon was the Zionist exponent of the "religion of labor," a secular version of a Hasidic teaching]. Since they came from a world of an ossified, circumscribed Judaism, they wanted to expand it to encompass with a great gesture all the phenomena of life, to insert them into

Judaism and overcome its narrow confinement.

So even though there's such a distance and discontinuation - I am
9 hours ahead of you – there is agreement, at least about a few
basic questions.

Perhaps most importantly, about David assigning me the task of making him into a Zionist and deeming our letters therefore worthy of posterity, I wrote: "You have to promise two things so that my work is not in vain. You have to become 'wise, old, and famous' and you have to come to Israel." While we joked and teased, there was an undercurrent: we were already challenging each other to think of our lives moving forward as bound to one another's, at least intellectually, if not yet romantically.

And was there, I wonder now, some fairly transparent displacement when I waxed poetic about *Madame Bovary*?

Isn't it a great book? Great in its original meaning. By the way, I
just read through it some days ago (as it is on the matriculation
exam) and found it as beautiful as always. Actually, I enjoy it
more every time I read it, it's the sort of book that grows and
enlarges with you every time you read in it; it doesn't stay behind
as just a beautiful memory. I really think it's one of the best books
I ever read and loved. Hurrah for books, as you said.

Perhaps to hide my tracks, I quickly veered off the subject of beauty and love and reported about Navah, who would be drafted two weeks later. The fiction that Navah was part of the correspondence continued for weeks, but, in reality, she never wrote David, not even once.

OCTOBER 6, 1970: RACHELI

My next letter on October 6, was ecstatic: my brother, Gil and his wife, Debbie, had just had a baby boy, Alon, born on October 5, the first member of the next generation of our family. Many years later, our son, Noam would be born on October 2 (1982) and our grandson, Abraham, on October 6 (2020). I was so thrilled that I drew a little cartoon of the occasion, with Gil and Debbie and baby on the right, my parents in the middle, with my brother Eran and me to their side. I was happy to report "he has non-Korati ears [all the ears in my family stick out]." I suppose I might have added – as we said many other times – that "they certainly knew where their children were."

OCTOBER 9, 1970: DAVID

As if to complicate the avowedly anti-religious stance of my October 2 letter, my next letter, written on Yom Kippur, announced that I was fasting for the first time. I explained myself by saying that it provided a conscious identification with Jews everywhere and at all times. Moreover, fasting creates a break with the past and the possibility of being born anew. However, two years later would be the last time I fasted on Yom Kippur. By then, I was in Jerusalem and Racheli and I went to several synagogues on foot in a scorching *hamsin*. Immediately upon breaking the fast, I became extremely ill and didn't recover for six weeks. The Israeli doctors couldn't figure out what was wrong, but I had an inkling: God, if he exists, was telling me not to worship him in that way.

On the question of atheism, my thoughts sounded remarkably like Racheli's long letter of October 2. Even if one believed that there is nothing outside of individual existence, it was still possible for the individual to identify with something beyond him or herself. That something is not God, but history:

> To deny atheism and to accept the burden of history is to commit oneself to one's people, to become something more than an individual. What I'm saying is that you, Racheli Korati, in spite of your kibbutz education, are really not an atheist.

More important (in retrospect) than my fasting or theologizing, was the following declaration:

> I find myself looking forward to your letters very much. They are my only real close tie to Israel. Keep the ink flowing, baby! In spite of our famous lack of agreement, we still manage to have something to say to each other.

OCTOBER 17, 1970: RACHELI

In the spirit of reflection and exploration of my Jewishness during the High Holidays, I attended a weekend seminar on Jewish thought for Simchat Torah. Preparing for it, I quoted, in a very long run-on sentence (trying to impress?), Søren Kierkegaard, the Sages of the Talmud and Carl Jung. All three sources reflected on the "Ages of Man" in terms of intellectual and spiritual development and made me question where I was on the continuum. I was particularly moved by this passage from Jung:

> The animus, just like the anima, exhibits four stages of development. He first appears as a personification of mere physical power – for instance, as an athletic champion, "muscle man" [like] Tarzan. In the next stage he possesses initiative and the capacity for planned action. The second stage can be portrayed as a "romantic" man – such as the poet Shelley or the "man of action," a figure like Ernest Hemingway, war hero, hunter, etc. The third phase, the animus becomes the "word" often appearing as a professor or clergyman. Finally, in his fourth manifestation, the animus is the incarnation of meaning. On this highest level he becomes a mediator of the religious experience whereby life acquires new meaning.

I was trying to locate myself along this progression: I wanted romance, I was enchanted by intellectual thought, and I was struggling to wrap my mind around spirituality-religiosity. I was also intrigued by the more psychological, or psycho-philosophical paradigms Jung employed. Pure philosophy or strict theology didn't resonate fully: perhaps this questioning already heralded my later turn as an adult towards the psychological in my professional life. I am intrigued, in hindsight, by my identification with the male animus as opposed to the female, anima, which Jung discussed in depth as well. Perhaps there is an invisible thread, which I am only seeing now, from my days on our kibbutz soccer team as the only girl to my later involvement with Jewish feminism as the author of *Women and Jewish Law*.

In conclusion, I wrote about the new chapter of my life that was about to unfold: I would spend a year working as a youth movement counselor (kibbutzniks had the option of a "year of service" as a youth movement counselor or working on a young, struggling kibbutz before their army service). I had it all mapped out: I was going to get placed in a youth movement branch (called a *"ken"* in Hebrew – literally, a nest) in Jerusalem. This would allow me to pursue various avenues for studying things Jewish. I fantasized about auditing courses at the Hebrew University and continuing to attend the monthly meeting of the Judaism study group I had been a part of in high school.

OCTOBER 18, 1970: DAVID

During the summer, Racheli had argued rather adamantly in defense of kibbutz education. I picked up that discussion in this letter. Kibbutz education was, no doubt, very effective at instilling good values, but what was lacking was the *historical* dimension. I situated it in a broader critique I had already formulated of the Zionist project to create a "normal" Jew in a normal state:

To be a Jew in Israel is as hard as to be a Jew in America because the temptations of the present (wealth, power) are overwhelming in the face of the small weak voice of the past (Jewish history). As long as Jews live in this world as Jews (I mean real Jews, with an organic connection to their history), then the idea of a normal existence is impossible. We are all awaiting the coming of the messiah – existing in a tension between the real and the possible.

What was missing in Zionism, which wanted a revolution, I thought, was a sense of the continuity of Jewish history. A.D. Gordon's religion of labor becomes meaningless unless it is linked to the history of mysticism and Hasidism, of which it was a dialectical product. It seems that I was already thinking historically.

But not so well clerically:

I lost a paper I had written 2 years ago on Hegel, Marx and Nietzsche (a small, modest effort). The professor, who is quite famous [Carl

Schorske, the distinguished European intellectual historian who had moved to Princeton] read it and miraculously liked it. He told me to send it to him when I needed recommendations for grad school. Oh well, another promising young historian bites the dust – yum.

It was pre-Xerox machines and, needless to say, pre-computers. If we copied our papers in those days, it was with carbon paper, but, alas, I didn't even have that. Assuming I was going to graduate school, I'd have to make it without Schorske's help. And, if I didn't get into graduate school: "I'll have no choice but to come to Israel."

OCTOBER 20, 1970: RACHELI

Given the long half-life of our letters -- it took 8-10 days for a letter to arrive, then a day or two to respond and another 8-10 for the return trip -- it was rather challenging to carry on a continuous conversation. But we certainly tried, so on October 20, I responded to David's letter about kibbutz education. I was fired up!

I got your letter yesterday and I have to reply immediately because you are wrong. You explained the term atheism as you use it – OK – and that clears up the picture. But then you write "in spite of your kibbutz education, you really are not an atheist." Objection! Kibbutz life, and thus the aims of kibbutz education, is the opposite of atheism and its implications. You need to <u>believe </u>to be a kibbutznik: believe in ideals, hopes and, more than that, you need to believe in the power of your belief, in your and your haverim's [comrades'] ability to build a life to fit a higher order of ideals. This is why kibbutz life has a lot, I think, in common with Judaism. They share a basic conception of man's life and as an accomplishment -- a materialization – of the "Kingdom of Heaven on Earth" and a social, human utopia in the kibbutz.

I was certainly a full-throated kibbutznik at the time. But I did see a fundamental flaw, exactly in what David and I were so preoccupied with, namely an authentic Jewish life: "What we lack in the kibbutz is a strong, vital connection to Am Yisrael, to our history... And this is what I – we - have to do for ourselves and for the kibbutz and, I believe and hope, for Judaism as well." I saw myself as on a path to infusing kibbutz life with a meaningful Jewishness, and I was clearly trying to recruit David to my mission. And yet, I recognized the doubts David expressed in his letters about Israel, Zionism and kibbutz life: "Having been fortunate enough to be born here – I don't know what to tell you, or if I have a right to – having things so much simpler for me."

I sound pretty ideologically dogmatic in this letter. I'm relieved to have turned out far less so.

OCTOBER 20, 1970: DAVID

We are all trying somehow to be Jewish in Berkeley. Paradoxically, the harder it is to be Jewish, the easier it becomes because you are conscious that anything you do that relates to Jewish history and tradition stands out from the white bread of American culture.

I think it is time that people realized how hard it is to be a Jew also in Israel. If you want to do something Jewish that the religious don't dig, they don't like you. If you want to do something that implies religion (or tradition), then everybody else doesn't like you. In some ways, it is easier to innovate in America – people seem to be more open to experimentation.

In hindsight, these observations point to my future path finding my Jewish identity through my work as an historian.

But not all the letters from these first few months of our correspondence were preoccupied with these weighty, even prescient, philosophical and cultural musings (or diatribes). There were also meteorological reports:

Yesterday was our first rain of the year – I love Berkeley when it rains. The clouds wrap themselves like blankets around the green hills and the sky turns dark blue and red at sunset. We may have much rain this year – will you send me Israeli sunshine in your letters?

I can say now, after nearly forty years of living Berkeley, that I remain in love with a Northern California winter.

OCTOBER 26, 1970: DAVID

I was now increasingly involved with the Radical Jewish Union, a group I defined for Racheli as "so-called New Left people who believe that you can be leftists and also pro-Israel." We met every Friday evening for dinner ("I was at my culinary best with an exquisite coq-au- vin!"), singing, and earnest discussion of matters Jewish and Zionist. I also threw myself into the group's newspaper, the Jewish Radical, to which I had made a self-important and rather juvenile contribution before my trip to Israel the previous spring. Now, I wrote an equally ambitious (might one even say a bit grandiose?) article about the early-twentieth-century Marxist Zionist theoretician, Ber Borochov (1881-1917), who was the idol of our group (it was an unwritten rule that everyone had to have a poster of Ber up on their college apartment walls – once I grew an Afro and a beard, I looked a bit like him). However, I doubted whether the Jewish question was one of class struggle, as Borochov thought. For my part, I thought that the correct position was philosophical anarchism, the rejection of bureaucratic sources of authority. I also enlisted Racheli to write as a foreign correspondent and she agreed that we could use her

Cover of *The Jewish Radical:* "Ber Borochov Memorial Edition"

earlier letter about kibbutz and Judaism (we never did, but she contributed later). In return, I promised to send her issues of our radical rag.

On Simchat Torah, we all repaired to the local Orthodox synagogue for "dancing and hooting around." There I ran into

Professor Richard Webster, with whom I planned to write my senior honors thesis in Jewish history. Webster, who was by training an Italian historian but read voraciously in Jewish history, was as eccentric as he was brilliant. He groused against the celebration: "That book [that is, the Torah] is opposed to everything Berkeley stands for. It's all about war and self-control." There it was: the whole Tanakh standing on one foot. I didn't bother to argue with him, but simply asked him, if so, what was he doing there? He wouldn't answer, but then his two cute kids ran up, so I suppose that was my answer.

OCTOBER 30, 1970: RACHELI

I began by poking some fun at David about a letter he had sent without including "Israel" in the address.

I found your letter – the one originally addressed to Racheli Korati, Kfar Ruppin (don't you think Racheli Korati is good enough by itself? I mean "kol yisrael haverim" [all of Israel are comrades] - so wouldn't they know who Racheli Korati is? And it's obvious every mailman can recognize it's written in Hebrew (what other language has such an odd appearance?) and thus conclude it is to be sent to Israel.

While David's letter exalted his coq-au-vin, mine bemoaned my fate taking the matriculation exams. I went into tedious details about each exam, but had enough self-awareness to conclude with "I guess all this is not terribly interesting but you must consider my mental state at present. I have 3 more exams next week - Bible, Hebrew Language, and Math."

I also reported, belatedly, about the Simchat Torah celebration I had attended at a religious community, which stands in interesting parallel to David's report about his experience:

I spent Simchat Torah in Kfar Etzyon. The Hakafot (dancing with the Torah) were great, the simcha [rejoicing] of these people - it's great. This is maybe one of the most important things we lack as a community: we secular kibbutzniks don't know how to rejoice together. I believe that in the early days of the kibbutz with 10 to 30 people in a kibbutz, they did know this (although you couldn't say they were generally happy people). I think their ability to rejoice was very closely connected with their hard life and suffering – physically and emotionally. Anyway, if you've ever been to such Hakafot – you know what I mean.

But in retrospect, an even more important aspect of this experience was my reaction to the separation of men and women in the synagogue. This might have germinated what I would now call my feminist awakening, which would take more than a decade to come to full bloom:

You have the great advantage (only in this case) of being a man – you may take part while I have to sit and watch! I'm sorry but no religious man has yet been able to convince me this separation is an integral part of prayer and is not a result of archaic concepts that haven't got sufficient justification, except that it is written and there are no great people today who are strong enough to change it. But that's their problem after all.

As the fifth P.S. among eight, I buried a clue about how I felt about David: "P.S. Devorah told me you wrote her. I must tell you that she did tell me what you told her not to tell me. You shouldn't have told her if you told her not to tell me – to begin with." We do not have that letter and, reconnecting with Devorah just as I was putting the finishing touches on this book, I asked if she remembered it. She doesn't, but it doesn't take a Sherlock Holmes to see what it was that neither of us was prepared to say out loud – or, more precisely, on paper.

I further covered my tracks by immediately jumping to the next P.S.: "Important: What do you think of Nixon's proposal [he proposed a five-point peace plan that the North Vietnamese rejected]? Is it going to get you out of the army?" The prospect of David being drafted hung like a sharpened saber over his head – and mine. It's probably impossible to convey, so many years later, what a chasm stood between the two worlds, but I certainly understood at the time that being drafted to the

US Army during the Vietnam War felt like a death sentence, while my draft was an adventure, with some physical and even mental challenges perhaps, but nevertheless, something to mostly look forward to.

NOVEMBER 4, 1970: DAVID

I was trying to figure out how to be in Jerusalem the following year, after graduating from Berkeley. The same Professor Webster whom I had run into at the Orthodox synagogue discouraged me from even entertaining the idea of getting a PhD at an Israeli university (he had just returned from a year's sabbatical at the Hebrew University with nothing but complaints). But a possible program emerged that would kill several birds with one stone: Hebrew Union College was interested in me since I was one of the few non-Orthodox American Jews who actually had pretty decent command of Hebrew. The first year of their rabbinical program took place in Jerusalem and might even come with some real financial support. But most importantly: a deferment from the American army!

In late 1970, the Vietnam War was an obsession with me and my friends. Every noon, we met for lunch on "The Terrace" on the UC Berkeley campus and debated the latest twists and turns of the war. Once we graduated, we would lose our student deferments and likely become cannon fodder, especially if we drew low numbers in the draft lottery (I got #67 out of 365, which was low enough to be drafted). We took to the streets to protest the war, not only because we thought it wrong and immoral, but also because we were in danger of becoming its casualties.

I hastened to assure Racheli that I had no intention of becoming a Reform Rabbi (God forbid!):

Now don't be in the least bit fooled by this: I certainly am the last one to become a rabbi, and I would cleverly slip out of their program after the first year (after that you have to return and cool your heels for five years in a seminary in some dreadful US city). In any case, how much better it would be to be in Jerusalem instead of Vietnam.

NOVEMBER 7, 1970: RACHELI

On November 7th I finished my matriculation exams and "to celebrate the end of the enslavement and the rebirth unto freedom – I slept 12 (twelve!) hours last night!" Furthermore, I announced: "The next step into the new era was, guess what – I started to read *Catch 22*!"

NOVEMBER 9, 1970: DAVID

[In Hebrew]
In silence, fall leaves
Upon the fields, the day is gone
Is she ambling on the paths?
Does she still remember the nights of love?

Inside the garden, singing flows
The sound of a sad harmonica
Is she still embroidering with a golden thread?
Does she still remember the nights of love?

Slowly, slowly, the weather vane spins
By the banks of the river, the weeping willow
Is she laughing or saddened?
Does she still remember the nights of love?

The village sleeps after a hard day's labor
Somewhere, a star has dimmed,
Is she standing by the door?
Does she still remember the nights of love?

This is my most beloved song in the album "Halokh Halkhah Ha-Hevraya" [The Gang Went Ambling Along – Russian dissidents' songs translated into Hebrew] which is undoubtedly my favorite

record of those I bought in Israel. The song is very sentimental but
also very Russian and that, of course, justifies the sentimentality.
And I also feel that this song resonates with my current mood (and
now I am becoming romantic – is that role alien to me?)

From hints of romance to my reading list: Tacitus, Thomas Mann,
Arthur Koestler, S.Y. Agnon ("The Lady and the Peddler," which
I claimed was not that hard in Hebrew), plus, most importantly,
Madame Bovary, which I loved but had to confess that I identified
with less than did Racheli. Fifty years later, as we were writing this
memoir, we decided to reread the novel to try to reconstruct why
it moved us so much. We were astonished at what a devastating
critique Flaubert leveled at the conventional romanticism of his day
and wondered whether we hadn't misread it in our youth.

NOVEMBER 21, 1970: RACHELI

To the news that David might be coming the next year, I
responded in my usual tongue-in-cheek manner (an obviously
unsuccessful disguise of how excited I was):

Don't forget to write me the flight number and time of arrival in
Lod airport. I promise I'll wait for you – I'll wear a green scarf
so that you can recognize me (with my short hair). What will
you use for self-identification (with your longer-than-my-hair)?
Seriously – I am waiting. When are you coming? You really think
you'll be here next year?

The day I get a letter from you saying you are positively coming
here (if I get one!?) I'll be unhappy – because I could have known
it a whole week earlier, if it weren't for the poor communication
writing letters gives you. To make up for this I'll take you seriously
and call you.

I actually meant this and we began to plan for a phone call in mid-
December. It would take a good three weeks for the letters to go back
and forth before we settled on a date and time.

David and I were by now in the habit of discussing at length in our letters what we were reading. We used these discussions not only as a way to formulate our emerging identities but also to gradually reveal ourselves to each other.

David, I finished Catch 22!!!

It's great. I finished at 1:00 AM at night and could not go to sleep. This always happens to me – I feel very strange when I finish a good book – what do you do now? I can't just go on to my business as if nothing happened – as I did before I knew this book. I used to have sort of a solution when I was young: I cried, but ... it's harder to do it now.

Crying at the end of a good book was, in fact, a treasured part of my childhood. Some books I checked out of the library repeatedly, my favorite being Janusz Korczak's *The Hope*, just so I could cry over them again.

NOVEMBER 21, 1970: DAVID

My most important reading accomplishment: I had finally finished Gershom Scholem's *Major Trends in Jewish Mysticism*, which I had been lugging around Israel the previous summer:

The man is so erudite that it's disgusting. I suppose that there are some who are geniuses enough to be truly original, while the rest of us are almost there but not quite over the magic boundary. The best we can do is to appreciate the true geniuses.

This was the first hint of what would later become a lifelong preoccupation with Scholem. He was the subject of my dissertation and first book, as well as my most recent book. Scholem had pioneered the study of Jewish mysticism, a field that earlier Jewish historians had despised. He succeeded in putting his subject at the very center of Jewish history and, in so doing, had become the most influential Jewish historian of the twentieth century. I was intrigued by how a secular historian like Scholem could find an intellectual path back to the Jewish religious tradition. Did I already have a hint that he would provide a model for me as a secular Jewish historian?

I had actually had a near encounter with Scholem when I was in Israel during the summer. While studying at the ulpan in July, I had gone with Navah to Jerusalem for Shabbat. On Saturday evening, after visiting a friend of hers, Navah and I discussed what to do next. She suggested that we visit an elderly couple whom she knew, but then dismissed the idea as probably tedious. Only much later did I discover that this elderly couple was Gershom and Fania Scholem! It would take nearly five more years until I met the great man.

As to Racheli's reading of *Catch-22*, I reacted in mock horror:

That book is the most subversive book ever written – if you really identify with it, you are destined to become as radical as we are on this side of the Atlantic. I dare say that that book is near-unto the Bible of this generation in America.

The third weekend of November our group of self-styled radicals traveled south to Los Angeles to take part in a confab of the Radical Zionist Alliance, a national network of Jewish student groups. I found myself in disagreement with most of them, especially with their doctrinaire Marxism. The real struggle, in both America and Israel, I thought, was against technology and soulless bureaucracy that atomized individuals. The correct response was not primarily politics or economics, but rather a counter-culture, which, I argued, was what authentic Judaism had always been.

This cultural emphasis is critical for American Jews. . . because the tendency of America is to destroy authentic ethnic cultures. To save themselves as human beings, they must save themselves as Jews. All power to the Jewish cultural anarchists (may they rise to power in both Israel and America)!

DECEMBER 1, 1970: DAVID

I had not only finished Gershom Scholem's *Major Trends*, but was now attempting to write about it, completing a paper comparing Heinrich Graetz and Scholem on their views of the Haskalah. Graetz, the preeminent German Jewish historian of the nineteenth century, had fully embraced the movement of Jewish enlightenment as the culmination of Jewish history and as the antithesis to the Kabbalah, which he called a "fungal crust on the essential kernel of Judaism." Scholem's position was more ambivalent and dialectical. I found myself attracted to his argument that Jewish mysticism provided the dialectical prerequisite for later developments in Jewish history, including Haskalah and Zionism. The failure of the mystical messianic movement of Shabbtai Zvi in the seventeenth century paved the ground for the collapse of rabbinic authority: "It is this ability to see the paradoxes and ambivalences in Jewish history that makes Scholem so great."

I was zeroing in on a subject for my senior honors thesis. Richard Webster suggested looking at Friedrich Nietzsche's influence on the Hebrew writer, Micha Yosef Berdichevsky. Webster was attracted to rightwing political and cultural movements (he wrote a book on the Italian proto-fascist, Gabriel D'Annunzio) and he thought that Berdichevsky might provide a window into a series of rightwing Zionist thinkers, like Vladimir Jabotinsky. I found that pretty interesting, although, in the end, my reading of Berdichevsky led in another direction.

DECEMBER 3, 1970: RACHELI

My plan to spend the year working in the youth movement in Jerusalem came to naught. I was posted instead to *Ken Borochov* (the Borochov branch of the youth movement) in Givatayim, a middle-class suburb outside of Tel Aviv. I totally missed the irony that Ber Borochov, for whom the branch was named, was one of David's idols who was frequently featured in the Jewish Radical. My Jerusalem dreams dashed, I tried to console myself with the knowledge that this branch was considered one of the crown jewels of the No'ar Ha-Oved youth movement. I would live with four other counselors in a communal apartment – or *Communa* - in an adjoining part of Ramat Gan, where rents were lower because it bordered on the ultra-orthodox Bnei Brak neighborhood.

The decision to send me there came as an utter shock:

Having never considered any alternatives besides Jerusalem, I was completely unprepared for the decision that I'll go to Tel Aviv. I had no time to argue (the last bus to Kfar Ruppin left a half hour later). I took 2 hours (the bus trip from Haifa to Kfar Ruppin) to recover from the shock by adopting a psychological tactic of making up a list of all the advantages there are in being a youth movement counselor in Tel Aviv. I'll still be able to go to the Tel Aviv University.

From that I jumped to what, at least in hindsight, was a dramatic realization, which would play out throughout my whole life:

I've decided - suddenly it occurred to me this moment – to study Jewish Studies in the university and not only this year, and give up for the time being the million other subjects I want to study. At a certain moment this morning, I realized that this was the "burning issue" for me right now – and that this field is the one where I feel I want to make the personal implications of the abstract apply to my life now.

Truth be told, I did not remember this "revelation" three years later when I arrived at UCLA and began attending Professor Amos Funkenstein's graduate seminar on medieval Jewish exegesis. It wasn't even a course I had contemplated, as I was set on getting myself a broad-based humanities education and also planned to take some courses on American history, to fill in big gaps in my Israeli education, which was both Jewish/Israeli-centric and Eurocentric. But David came home after the first seminar and told me I MUST attend, that Funkenstein was the most brilliant person he had ever met. I gave it a try, despite being an entering freshman. I thought that Uda's classes and the study group equipped me to be a silent auditor in the seminar. I was hooked and, not terribly surprising, could not remain silent for long.

But my Tel Aviv University dreams never materialized. As it turned out, either work for the youth movement was more demanding than I had anticipated or I was lazier than I wanted to acknowledge. Either way, I did not do any studying that year. I do remember making one visit to the university campus, taking three different buses from the Communa in Ramat Gan at the eastern edge of Tel Aviv to the university north of the city. I eyed the students enviously, while reclining luxuriously on the wide green lawn, but I couldn't screw up the courage to enter a lecture hall. *Next time*, I told myself, *I'm just getting the lay of the land this time.* But I never came back. I suspect it did seem out of reach for a kibbutznik just three months out of high school.

DECEMBER 8, 1970: DAVID

I returned from Los Angeles to find several of Racheli's letters. This led me to ruminate on the advantages and disadvantages of letter writing:

> *You can often think out what you want to say and say that more precisely and boldly than in conversation. On the other hand, when I read your letters, I often wonder if the nuances I pick up you intend to put there.*

The pot would have been justified in calling the kettle black: I was no doubt as guilty of embedding as many hidden, between-the-lines messages as she was. And I was anything but bold in expressing what I was really feeling.

"Let me conclude that we should utilize the advantages of writing by continuing to write, but overcome its disadvantages by Mr. Bell's invention." Our plan to connect by phone on December 13 was progressing. It was complicated. There were only three phones on the kibbutz: one in the kibbutz office, only available for kibbutz business during the workday, one in the dining room with zero privacy and a cacophony of voices in the background, and one for members to use for personal calls, located in a mosquito-infested shack. The plan was for Racheli to call me collect at the appointed time and, because international calls were prohibitively expensive in those days, it would have to be a very short conversation ("hello, can you hear me? I can hear you ..."). The call, when it actually happened, appears to have been pretty frustrating and even alienating compared to our letters. Mr. Bell's invention would not advance our relationship.

But when it came to our letters, I confessed that coming home to find a letter from Racheli made me very happy. And, so I wrote:

> Let me be honest: I wouldn't be thinking much about coming to Israel next year except for you being there. We didn't get to know each other that well in the five weeks or whatever last summer, but, somehow, I feel close enough to you to say that it would be nice to be together next year.
>
> A lot can, of course, happen here but a lot can also happen through letters (n'est-ce pas?). Well, I'll end on that awkward note . . . we're off to demonstrate in San Francisco against Vice-President Ky of South Vietnam (let's hope my head is no more bashed in at the end of the day than it already is now).

"Nice" was a pretty lame way to express my affections.

DECEMBER 30, 1970: RACHELI

I, too, found our December 13 call unsatisfying and that dissatisfaction may account for the silence on both of our ends for two weeks after it. But if "Mr. Bell's invention was no substitute for letters," I now had astonishing news for something even better than written correspondence. In letters, about five times larger than the usual, I wrote:

> I never would have dreamed of a dream materializing so fast and easy. It is almost positive that in two weeks I will be nowhere else BUT IN (YES!) AMERICA!!!
>
> The United Jewish Appeal (UJA) is sending 4 "shelling subjects" from Kfar Ruppin to America on a tour aimed at helping rich American Jews give up their money and give it to ISRAEL. You know all that blah-blah. But who cares for that part of the journey?

The UJA delegation from Kfar Ruppin included me, my mother, a man named "Czech" who was a colorful, idiosyncratic character introduced to our audiences as "in charge of security at the kibbutz," and a handsome 10th grade boy with a sweet smile and a twenty-five-word English vocabulary. I was so excited I couldn't write much more:

> *You will forgive me, I can't write about anything else today. If I manage to calm down a bit I'll write soon – I have a lot of things I'd like to write but presently prefer to wait till we can talk.*
> *SEE YOU SOON!*
> *Sooner than I ever expected! LOVE, Racheli*

Chapter 2

CALIFORNIA DREAMING
January-April 1971

JANUARY 5, 1971: RACHELI

Now I had to wait impatiently until David would receive my December 30 news and then reply. I wrote at the moment when I thought he might be reading the news: "According to my calculations you should be reading my previous letter now – 2:30 PM your time. So, I'm starting to count the five days I have to wait till I can be really be sure you know you can expect an Israeli invasion soon."

Meanwhile, I had become anxious due to the long break in our correspondence:

David, has anything happened? It's almost a whole month since you last wrote. I don't know what to say – I sort of lost contact with you since we talked. Do we have to wait till we talk to start writing again, as we did before? I hope for a letter and get disappointed twice a day when mail comes at 10:00 and at 2:00.

Having revealed my worries, I quickly returned to the safety of "business as usual," telling David about my work in the youth movement, my doubts about bridging between anarchism and Jewishness, my matriculation exam grades, and what I was reading (Kierkegaard and a book of philosophical-ideological conversations among young kibbutzniks). But then I returned to the excitement about seeing each other: "I've got a million other things to write that I would rather <u>SAY</u>." I signed off more boldly than before: "Much, Much Love, Racheli."

JANUARY 5 – JANUARY 14, 1971: DAVID

A bombshell letter from Racheli that, out of the blue, she would be coming to visit me in a couple of weeks, while on a United Jewish Appeal fundraising trip. I responded with "understatement:" "WHEN ARE YOU COMING, HOW LONG CAN YOU STAY? THAT'S THE GREATEST NEWS IN A LONG, LONG TIME!!!!!!!!!" I suggested that she abscond from the tour and hide out in Berkeley the whole time. She could give her "propaganda speeches" to the Radical Jewish Union, instead of the United Jewish Appeal. She could also visit Professor Webster's Jewish history seminar: "Brilliant, but loony as two insane asylums. He told me that if he were reincarnated, he would like to come back as a virus. Why? Think of all the opportunities for travel – it's a freeloader's paradise!" I also informed her that I had started teaching Hebrew at Berkeley High School and that she was invited to give a visiting lecture in my class.

But so as not to be taken too seriously: "The only way I can understand this happening is theologically: somebody up there is pulling strings. We've got the Almighty and the Zionist movement on our side."

JANUARY 8, 1971: RACHELI

The plan was confirmed: "It's absolutely, positively, really real – I'm coming over." I was to arrive in the US on January 26 or so, and reach California less than two weeks thereafter. The trip included two or three days in Berkeley, when we were to speak to students at the university and perhaps some other group. I recently found a clipping from *The Jewish Bulletin of Northern California*, describing our talk to the Young Adult Division of the Jewish Community Federation in San Francisco. But what is memorable is the fact that the UJA staff were very generous and agreed to let me book a flight from Los Angeles to New York via San Francisco instead of the original direct LAX - JFK flight. This allowed me to return to Berkeley for three or four days at the end of our tour and spend more time with David.

It should have been a dream come true, a sensational explosion of romance and passion. But it wasn't. We – or at least I – were not ready. Our time together was intense but still totally chaste, full of deep conversations and new experiences for me, but still utterly platonic. I got to hike in the Berkeley Hills and catch a glimpse of the landscape David loved so much. I fell in love with it too. He introduced me to his hevre in the Radical Jewish Union. While I suspected that for him the most important aspect was getting his close friends to give me the once over, for me, it was a thrilling immersion in their world of activism and intellectual ferment. I even got to work with them on the laborious cut-and-paste process of laying out an issue of the Jewish Radical, and was included in their "Toilers for this Issue" column. He also took me to a study session at Rabbi Pinchas Lipner's home (Lipner, a newcomer to the Bay Area, had established an Orthodox Jewish Day School in 1969). It felt a little bit like our study group at Uda's but, more importantly, it provided me with the necessary background and personal connection for understanding the intense passion behind the RJU's sit-in at the San Francisco Jewish Community Federation that would take place at the end of April of that year. Without that, I suspect I would have had no clue why those hevre were so hot under the collar about Jewish education.

Novices at love as we were, we were unable to explicitly talk about our feelings and our relationship. I was at once relieved and disappointed that David arranged for me to spend the nights at the apartment of a female friend. I am sure I would not have known how to handle myself if he had offered me his bed or his couch, even if framed as just "crashing at his place," with no one speaking of "sleeping together." In some ways this was a setback: after the visit we both stayed mum for three months about our disappointment. Yet, in hindsight, I wonder if this frustrating visit was a blessing in disguise. I know I was not ready for a sexual relationship at that point and, had we tried it in February, perhaps it would have been a much greater debacle than just the repressed emotions. And, if so, it might have nipped our love in the bud.

JANUARY 14, 1971 -- MARCH 2, 1971: DAVID

There was a six-week hiatus in my correspondence, including the time when Racheli came twice to visit in Berkeley. It is hard for me, even now, to write about that visit. It was very intense and, as she has written, an introduction to the wonders of Berkeley and the Radical Jewish Union. However, despite the clear build-up in our letters of the previous four months, we were unable or unready to declare what is, no doubt, obvious to any reader of these letters. If I had had more confidence in myself as a lover, I would have said to her, quite simply: "I think I'm falling in love with you. Do you feel the same way?" As Joni Mitchell sang in her famous song: "Tears and fears and feeling proud, to say I love you right out loud." Such a declaration, perhaps on the tip of my tongue, would have to wait until it ripened.

Readers may well wonder how we could have been so tentative and, yes, repressed, while all around us, the sexual revolution was taking place. Our story here is quite at odds with what most of our peers remember of that time when people often had sex before they knew much more about each other than their names. We, too, at least theoretically, embraced liberating sex from old fashioned inhibitions and constraints. So, it is with some wonder that we look back at the story of our love as one out of joint with the times, but also one that matched who we were, reigning ideology be damned.

We now realize that we were nineteenth-century romantics at heart.
A slow epistolary love story suited us better.

FEBRUARY 6, 1971: RACHELI

As soon as I got home from the trip, I wrote a letter full of
emotions, but not about us and the visit. It seems I channeled all of
my erotic energy into the wildflowers that welcomed me back home:

> *"On our way back home" [referencing the Beatles song, which
> is, of course, a love song] all the way from Tel Aviv to Afula.
> Everywhere, everything – rich but not heavy green, and your
> eyes caught, almost hypnotized, by sparkling, bright spots of the
> reddest red – all this against very clear, light blue sky ... kalaniyot
> [anemones].*

Throughout my childhood, I had a passionate attachment to the red
anemones that bloomed in the hills surrounding Kfar Ruppin and
all around Israel. So much so, that during the year I spent in Boston,
when we had an assignment in our English class to write a "romantic
poem," I wrote one about these flowers. I wish I could remember it.
I'm afraid it was rather corny, linking the red flowers to the blood
spilled by Israelis defending the country in its many wars. The only
line I remember is "children picked the anemones/ The eyes of the
spring."

To bring the scene to life for David, I picked one anemone and
pressed it. Drying flowers in our homemade presses was a big part of
my childhood. It began in first grade when our teacher had each of
us pick one flower, press it and send it with a short letter to a "Jewish
child in the Galut [diaspora or exile]," asking him or her to be our
pen-pal. Now David was my "pen-pal in the Galut." I sent him the
flower, inserted inside a Bible. We still have the flower, but, alas, not
the Bible. Amazingly, it has retained a slightly browned shade of its
original glory.

Once I poured my heart out through the anemones, I did hint at my feelings about the visit: "I feel, I don't have a word for it - disconnected, maybe. Everything seems discontinued, cut, between today and a week and a half ago. I feel further away, less connected, than I did before the proof came that you were still real." But then I got scared by my own honesty and undercut it with a comment – in Hebrew – "Nonsense!" And then, again, back to being truthful, "But I miss you, and it's more real now."

FEBRUARY 26, 1971: RACHELI

Soon thereafter, I spent a week at Kibbutz Gadot in the Hullah Valley picking grapefruits. I waxed rather poetic about it:

It's fascinating how much satisfaction with pleasure, with calmness, you achieve working very hard – physically – using all your energy, strength; to complete exhaustion. I once talked with

my Abba about working in the Dining Room – I said I enjoyed
it (for a while) because you had to work very fast and very hard,
put everything into it. And you get "used up" completely. He was
smiling, saying something that said to me that he was thinking:
"I know where my children are."

In a short story my father had written in English in 1946 (his Hebrew
was still limited to the quotidian), which I first read just a few years
ago (long after he died), he expressed these sentiments about manual
labor in the masculine, muscular language of Ernest Hemingway,
whom he aspired to emulate. Describing his protagonist, M., turning
the soil over with his *turiyah* (a large hoe) he wrote:

> The land was a fierce, strange woman who will yield to a strong
> and merciless hand only; which, when ploughed, overturned,
> cut through by countless aqueducts and furrows, tortured and
> beaten, gave away its mysterious secrets, its abundant riches.

> It was great to be one of these to whom this land yielded, to whom
> Nature lowered its gracious, proud head, and to become one
> with it, feel the hidden pulse, touch the ever vibrating, sensual
> nerves of it. A man could become drunk with the morning air,
> the stillness reigning around, the faint splash of the distant river.

Years later, in the 1960's, he wrote a tongue-in-cheek piece in Hebrew
in the kibbutz newsletter, describing the "exotic habits" of the
inhabitants of Kfar Ruppin, and signed it Ernest Hemingway. When
my mother read it, not knowing he was the author, she chuckled and
then asked him: "But who is this Ernest the Mini-Goy?' In Hebrew,
without the vowels, the two words look identical.

Recollecting that conversation with my father and reporting that
Uda was going to be giving a talk in Kfar Ruppin about "Searching
for Jewish Identity among Second Generation Kibbutzniks," led me
to broader reflections: "The trouble with Kfar Ruppin is not enough
of the second-generation experience that [search]." Uda had also sent
me a booklet on *The Halakha and Contemporary Society*, which I
found exciting, quoting its key argument in Hebrew:

We will not be mistaken, then, to say that Jewish nationalism rose out of confrontation between secular nationalism and traditional Judaism, the confrontation between the individual world-view of a thinking person vis-a-vis the traditional world-view of Judaism. Only someone who is not indifferent to the world of Judaism, whether by identification or engagement with it gains the right to be counted as part of Jewish nationalism.

MARCH 2, 1971: DAVID

In my first letter after her visit, I, too, avoided the storm of emotions that remained repressed just under the surface, although my salutation – "Dearest Racheli" -- said perhaps more than I consciously intended.

Nu, has your pen run out of ink? I still can't believe that you were here and I keep expecting you to drop in next weekend. Not much new in the land of long hair. I was accepted to graduate school in Berkeley and they're even going to give me some money! So, I can stay here ... if I don't get drafted. I was also accepted to Hebrew Union College, which means I can go there instead ... which means Israel! I haven't made any decisions yet. The absurd thing is how much we live in the future, without concentration on the present. So, for the next few months, I'll focus on the present and to hell with the future.

There actually was something new "in the land of long hair." Muki Tsur, one of the foremost ideologues and historians of the kibbutz movement, especially in its tumultuous early days, visited our group:

Do you know that he studied with Gershom Scholem for four years? That's real contact with the horse's mouth. He had some very interesting stories to tell about Scholem and Buber and all those characters. Muki is a very unusual and perceptive kind of person. He made a great impression, particularly on those people who don't like Israelis generally (well, I guess I fall into that group, although I have to admit to liking <u>a very few</u> Israelis).

What I was referring to was a remarkable talk that Muki gave in Harry Edwards' sociology class. Edwards, one of the organizers of the 1968 Black Power demonstration of athletes at the 1968 Mexico City Olympics, was known as one of the more radical professors on the Berkeley campus, and his class attracted a lot of student radicals. Ken Bob, one of the members of the RJU (and a close friend to this day) was in that class and convinced Edwards to invite Muki to speak on the kibbutz. Muki began in his quiet, understated but eloquent way, when one student tried to disrupt his talk. Edwards was clearly captivated by Muki. A huge man, he stood up, towering over our Israeli friend by at least a foot, and vehemently informed the class that anyone who dared interrupt Muki would have to deal with him later. Muki proceeded to captivate not only Edwards, but the whole class.

MARCH 14, 1971: RACHELI

Part of my homecoming was making my room in the Communa more special, more "in my own image," which by now was heavily influenced by the psychedelic colors and designs in *Yellow Submarine* and the cover of the *Sgt. Pepper's Lonely Hearts Club Band* album. I reported to David: "I finished (a week ago) painting my room – after painting the walls lilac-purple, I painted the furniture (door, window, tables, chairs, book shelves) dark blue. I like it a lot, though a lot of people don't. But that's their problem." A little while later I sent David a picture of me painting my room (wearing a rain hat, which I recall was bright yellow, to protect my hair from flying paint drops, and a by-now ragged but still beloved Newton High School P.E. T-shirt), and another one resting after my labors on the Communa's porch.

Evidently on a bit of a tear with paints, I also extended my artwork to the youth movement branch clubhouse: "I have to paint the wall 'psychedelically' in a music room the kids set up really beautifully, with equipment for recording and earphones for listening to music."

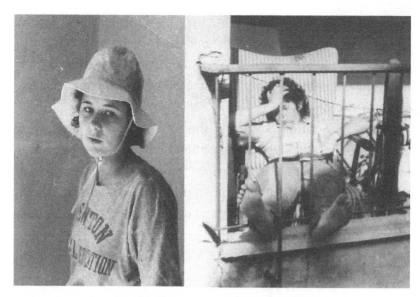

Painting my room and its aftermath.

As to the public's reception of my artwork, I suppose by "a lot of other people" who didn't like it I meant my Communa buddies, since we didn't really have many visitors. Mostly these were fellow counselors from other branches and, on somewhat embarrassing occasions, our parents. But one visitor stood out. It was on the day I had returned from a week-long trip to the Sinai, which meant no showers. I took a particularly long one to scrape off the sand and salt from the Red Sea. As I emerged with one towel wrapped around my body and another on my head, one of my Communa roommates warned me: "There is a rabbi here to see you." I made a bee-line for my room, passing behind him so fast I hoped he didn't catch a glimpse of my immodest attire. I changed and emerged from my room, dumbfounded to find Rabbi Chaim Druckman seated at our dining room table. Druckman had been one of the venerated teachers of the Jewish study group of my high school senior year. He taught us Hasidic tales, biblical homilies, and a lot of *niggunim* (wordless Jewish melodies)

What on earth was he doing there? How had he found my

address? What was on his mind visiting an unmarried, secular kibbutznik in her apartment in the mid-afternoon, albeit on the edge of his world, the ultra-orthodox neighborhood of Bnei Brak. I leave it to your imagination … but I don't think he was intent on sharing pearls of Torah wisdom.

We were a rather odd lot in the Communa. Two of us were born-and-bred kibbutzniks while the other three were graduates of the youth movement from various towns around Israel. I shared a room with the only other woman, Ruti. She was a nice enough roommate; after all, she let me paint our room and furniture those colors. But I don't think I remember her actually ever coming to the *ken* to take charge of any activities. I suspected that she spent most of her time roaming around the fashionable streets of Tel Aviv hoping a photographer or talent agent would notice her and offer her a modeling contract. The three guys were each quirkier than the next, and we had uproarious nights poking fun at each other, at our "mission," and running through the more peculiar among our kids at the ken.

Dudi, the other true kibbutznik, was my closest friend in the Communa. I suppose we could have become a couple if he hadn't been in love with a Canadian volunteer on his kibbutz named Suzanne, the same name as the girl in James Taylor's "Fire and Rain," which he played endlessly. And I, of course, was in love with David, even though neither of us had said it out loud. I guess that one of the things Dudi and I had in common was North American kibbutz volunteers! Dudi and I kept in touch very intermittently over many years; there was always a sadness about our widely divergent life trajectories (he returned to his kibbutz after his army service, worked as a carpenter and lived as "an ordinary kibbutznik") and a wistful remembering of our Communa days.

Communal apartments like ours were scattered throughout the country to house youth movement counselors. We shared expenses, meals, chores and endless conversation and horsing around. Living in the Communa was eye-opening for me: I marveled at how close I felt to the fellow counselors with whom I actually had little in common besides our work and a shared living situation. It was actually a surprising contrast with my feelings about the kids I grew up with on Kfar Ruppin. We had been together since the day our mothers brought us home from the hospital. We had shared so many experiences: some exhilarating, many amusing and some, especially in hindsight as a mother myself, rather disturbing if not outright terrifying. But by the time I left the kibbutz and my class, my connection to my cohort had become rather tenuous, our relationships flat, full of shared memories but little to talk about now. In the Communa, I discovered some of the magic of a close-knit group:

Living in the Communa has been very important in terms of developing my thoughts and feelings about kibbutz life. I'm sure I said this before, but it amazes me how much I love these people, knowing that, under any other conditions and situations, we would never have become closer than the superficial, none of us would have chosen any of the others as a friend. And knowing each other so well, I still wouldn't choose them for my friends, but somehow living together has gotten it so we simply and honestly love each other. Something very beautiful shines around each one, around all of us when we are together. I wanted you to meet them – hoping you'll be able to sense these feelings, hoping you could feel, share a little of my love.

While I was steeped in this experience of camaraderie and dreaming of building a life based on it, David had a similarly deep connection with his friends in Berkeley. I felt we were each, in our own sphere, creating the building blocks for an intimate group of friends living together.

MARCH 21 (?) AND MARCH 28, 1971: DAVID

For the first three weeks or so of March, it appears that I did not write, for reasons that I cannot reconstruct, except that perhaps I was busy writing papers at the end of the winter quarter (although I never failed to report to Racheli about my academic doings). During the break between winter and spring quarters, I enjoyed the onset of spring:

> Rossini on the record player. His overtures fit the day, which was hot and sunny and Italian. We rode our bikes to the botanical gardens, which were lush with California poppies (almost as beautiful as the Israeli anemones), the hills emerald green, and the sun reached down and baked our bodies. It was a day for the eyes and the ears and especially the nose (when you can smell the flowers and the grass and the trees, you know that spring has arrived). Right outside my window, I can smell the lilac, which is warm and sweet. If I have to choose between cold, winter days, huddling by a warm fire, and beautiful, hot spring, even though I love both, I think I would choose spring. Somehow, life seems more intense, more exhilarating, when the sun burns away winter's misty doubts.

And doubts there were. I wrote of agonizing about whether to take up a prestigious offer (with fellowship) from Princeton, stay in Berkeley, or "heed the biblical call, gird up my loins like Abraham (or whoever) and go the Land of Canaan." The latter would have been through Hebrew Union College, only really a live option if the long arm of Uncle Sam threatened to snatch me for Vietnam. Professor Webster wanted me to go to Princeton, which didn't really have any Jewish historians, but, being there, I would be able to study with Gerson Cohen at the Jewish Theological Seminary. By now, however, Berkeley was in my blood, so I was very tempted to stay, even though it was also not a place to study Jewish history:

> In Berkeley you can live a truly balanced life between intellectual activities at the university, Jewish activities, because it is such a close community, and even lots of physical exercise and contact with nature. It seems to me that one should have all of these and not let one dominate the rest.

Would that be possible on kibbutz, I wondered?

I had a curious sense of history perhaps repeating itself:

Did I tell you how my father almost went to Palestine in 1931, except he got a fellowship to do a PhD and stayed in Berkeley? If I come next year to Israel, I might stay, which wouldn't be the worst thing in the world. However, I wonder if it would be a mistake in terms of what I want to do (Jewish history, European intellectual history, etc.). But if I delay, the same thing may happen to me as to my father. And I'm not so sure about the future of the academic profession in this country.

Racheli had sent me two presents, which didn't make my decision about the next year any easier:

Thank you, <u>very, very</u> much for the Tanakh and the kalanit. The flower is now hanging above my bed and the Bible is on the bookshelf next to it. What I'd really like to do next year is study the book in the land where the red flower is actually growing, instead of sitting behind plastic on my wall. I was very moved by the quotation ("Cast your bread upon the waters ...") you had me read in the Tanakh. What's so beautiful is that we don't even need to say things ourselves – all we have to do is refer to a book written long before the age of Aquarius.

I was by now fully immersed in my study of M.Y. Berdichevsky, whose weird philosophy of Jewish history juxtaposed ethics and the book against nature, strength and the sword. His call for a "new Hebrew man" in place of diaspora Jews was fascinating, on the one hand, but also deeply repellant, on the other. He wanted to overthrow all of Jewish tradition, starting with the Bible, in favor of a subterranean "counter-history" of militarism and Nietzschean "vitalism." Although Berdichevsky was not a political activist, his views both influenced and reflected the development of the Zionist "negation of the Diaspora." I found my own ambivalence about contemporary Israeli culture playing out in Berdichevky's recondite writings from the end of the nineteenth century. Here was a writer calling for a Jewish revolution, but was it one to which I could really subscribe? After all, I was on a journey of discovery of the Jewish tradition, not rejection of all of it. In any case, just deciphering his texts was challenge enough. I thought that my Hebrew was pretty good by now, but his was a style that preceded the emergence of Hebrew as a modern spoken language. I was reading furiously, but my progress was painfully slow.

In between these existential and intellectual struggles, I nevertheless found time for less serious matters. In response to Racheli's report on painting her room in the Communa, I wrote in mock horror:

> *The color of your room sounds absolutely hideous!!!!! I hope you weren't inspired by the painting job I did in my apartment [I had painted my room the previous fall a garish blue and orange]. Hey, maybe you've been smoking something you shouldn't (you clean-cut kibbutz kids ought to know better than to play around with psychedelic Israeli hashish).*

APRIL 4 – APRIL 13, 1971: RACHELI

We both needed to make some fateful decisions about the next year or two: David about graduate school and me about the army. By April 13, I had heard that he had chosen Berkeley and I applauded his choice: "I'm for Berkeley too!"

Meanwhile, I announced my army plans: "I've decided to go to the Nachal." The Nachal is a branch of the army that allows youth movement kids to serve together with their *ken* cohort and spend a good part of their army service on kibbutzim. They serve on a well-established one and also a newer, young kibbutz, plus a stint on a *he'achzut*, an army outpost in a border area which is organized like a mini-kibbutz. "This means I will be drafted sometime in early fall 1971. I'll find out this Thursday when I get to give freedom a two-year divorce."

APRIL 15, 1971: DAVID

In early April, I went to Los Angeles for Passover with my family. While there, I engaged in intensive discussions with our compatriots in the Jewish Radical Community. I also got to know a number of very impressive young rabbis. One, in particular, Moshe Adler, gave "a beautiful defense of his position on halakhah. Such people give me faith in the possibility of faith." I also got to know Adler's wife at the time, Rachel Adler, who two years later would write "The Jew Who Wasn't There," the most important essay of the nascent movement of Jewish feminism. The way Rachel challenged Moshe on theological matters was exhilarating to watch. While I never ended up adopting Moshe Adler's enlightened form of Orthodoxy, Rachel Adler's feminism would shape much of both my and Racheli's later academic work, not to speak of our politics.

I was less enthused by our family Passover seder: "it didn't have much spirit and degenerated into an argument about Soviet Jews. I tried to direct the argument in such a way as to apply the lessons of the Haggadah to the question of the Soviet Jews, but it didn't work." I can't recollect what the argument might have been. My uncle Shimon, who, with my aunt Frania, had spent the war in the Soviet Union, first in a Siberian labor camp and then in Uzbekistan, would surely have been arguing for militant action on behalf of Soviet Jews. While Shimon and I had earlier disagreed vehemently about the Vietnam War (he was in favor, I opposed), it is likely that we formed an alliance on this issue. In any event, the RJU staged a number of demonstrations as well as published articles in the Jewish Radical as part of the movement to liberate the Soviet Jews.

MAY 1, 1971: RACHELI

On May 1, I wrote to David in Hebrew. I generally switched to Hebrew when I wanted to write a more emotional, poetic letter. This one, inspired by the end of spring, contained reflections on youth and death:

The expression "plucked in his youth" is very graphic: meaning, as you probably know, died at a young age – plucked in his youth: "Be'ibo = be'avivo" means in his springtime. Just like spring in this country. It adorns itself like a youth with flowers and blossoms and then the hamsin comes: its flowers wilt, its green turns yellow, the blue of its sky becomes a pale, bright blue, almost blinding, nearly translucent, and heat spreads through everything. Suffocating, boiling-hot air, heavy and wrapped in the sweet smell of a wilting izdarechet [Indian lilac tree] weighing and pressing on you; a current of heat spreads throughout your body - burning to push and press out through the skin, it almost drips off the ends of your fingers on your limp, hanging hands, fatigued, so heavy, on your side.

That's it: a funeral for Spring was held last week. The backdrop: yellowing fields with only burning-red spots, almost melting in the heat, of poppies dotting them. This is the summer which in the Bible – in the Book of Ruth – is called "The beginning of the barley harvest" (Ruth 1:22).

The Song of Songs is about the flowering of first love, in tandem with the first flowers of spring. The Book of Ruth portrays a mature love, symbolized by the ripening of the grain. So, it's tempting to read back into this letter the awareness that our relationship was maturing. But I had no inkling of the struggle David was having with himself to finally put his feelings into words and write his dramatic letter on the third of May.

TO SAY I LOVE YOU RIGHT OUT LOUD
May-August 1971

MAY 3, 1971: DAVID

Once back in Berkeley, I was swept up by several political actions. On April 24, the Radical Jewish Union organized a Jewish contingent to the San Francisco March Against the Vietnam War. We were joined by a group from the Jewish Radical Community in LA and, all together, we numbered some 100 people, carrying signs with biblical quotations. We were, of course, vastly outnumbered by other marchers – there were about a quarter million people marching from the financial district of San Francisco to Golden Gate Park. But it was an exhilarating experience to be there as Jews against the war.

Jewish contingent at anti-war demonstration April, 1971
(From left: David, Bradley Burston, Larry Tishkoff, unidentified)

An even more consequential action took place the following Friday and Saturday (April 30-May 1). One of the issues that our group embraced was Jewish education. In our view, the American Jewish community did not invest in intellectually exciting Jewish education, so that most Jewish children fled the synagogues' religious schools as soon as they fulfilled their Bar or Bat-Mitzvah obligation. Several members of the RJU had been educated in Jewish day schools and they argued that such an immersion experience could revolutionize Jewish life. We discovered that the San Francisco Jewish Federation devoted very little of its budget to education. So, we formed a "Jewish Education Coalition" (really a front for the RJU) and demanded that they change their priorities. Needless to say, we got no response.

Well, we were children of the '60s, so it was time for direct action: a sit-in at the Federation offices on Bush Street in San Francisco. We planned the operation with "military" precision: one other member of the group and I distracted the receptionist with earnest questions and amusing banter while the forty-three other members of the group charged through the unguarded front door. Here's how I reported it to Racheli:

> *The thing was beautifully organized; we occupied the offices at 11:30 in the morning and announced that we were staying for Shabbat. The rich guys came running in and told us to leave or they would call the police. We got into a very interesting debate with them about what it meant for them to be Jewish and what it meant for us. Then we told them that we wouldn't leave until they met our demands. They backed down and didn't call the cops. We then had a terrific Shabbat dinner (which we had brought) and very good singing. Lots of people from the community came to see what we were doing, including a number of rabbis [one of these rabbis was Wolfe Kelman, a central figure in the Conservative movement and the father of Levi and Naami, now two of our closest friends]. We slept in the offices Friday night and then decided to leave after Havdalah. We got pretty good press. I was interviewed on TV, radio and in the newspapers since I was one of the machers in the group. Then, the next day was Israel Independence Day and we showed up with leaflets and Jewish Radicals and I was given permission to make a statement in front of the crowd, which was a waste of time since they were all 85 and couldn't hear a damn thing.*

Those "rich guys" who "rushed in" to have us arrested but ended up in a debate with us were led by Mel Swig, the son of Ben Swig, one of San Francisco's wealthiest hoteliers. The Swigs were typical representatives of the highly assimilated wealthy elite of the San Francisco Jewish Community. They were often intermarried and sat on the Boards of Trustees of Catholic institutions (there was a tight alliance between Jews and Catholics in San Francisco) and donated very generously to hospitals, Golden Gate Park, museums and the Opera. Mel Swig was so befuddled that he didn't think that either Jewish education or Jewish identity were the "business of the Jewish Federation."

The Jewish Radical's article about the Sit-In

This was the RJU's most dramatic political action, although certainly not the only one. But it also had unintended consequences. There were only two Jewish day schools in the Bay Area at the time: the non-denominational Brandeis Community School and Rabbi Pinchas Lipner's Hebrew Academy (now defunct). We had developed a relationship with Lipner (I had taken Racheli to a study session with him when she visited Berkeley in February). But shortly after our sit-in, we became increasingly suspicious of him. Not only was his orthodoxy much too extreme for us, but his rightwing politics on Israel clashed sharply with the RJU's position. In later years, after Racheli and I returned to live in Berkeley, I came to really regret our support for Lipner: when we organized a protest against Israel's heavy-handed response to the First Intifada in 1988, Lipner took out an ad in the local Jewish attacking us in fulminating language.

With all this excitement to report in my May 3 letter, I finally came to the real matter that was on my mind:

But now I guess I can't avoid what I really want to write about, which is the real reason it has taken me so long to write since my last letter [April 15]. I guess I am a little dissatisfied with the kind of letters we have been writing to each other. While I am, of course, interested in what you are doing (and maybe you are even interested in how I've been wasting my time), I feel like we should be saying a lot more and perhaps talking about how we feel about each other and where things are going to go from here. To be honest, I never really wrote to you about how I felt about your visit here [in February] and you never told me exactly how you felt.

I think I felt much closer to you this time than I did last summer and I really sense a growth and development in our relationship. But I also felt a kind of awkwardness that I can't describe – perhaps due to differences in age and experiences and the environments that we both grew up in. I know that I feel closer to you than to any other girl I know now, and I feel very deeply the ten thousand miles that separate us.

Does this make any sense, Racheli, or should it have been left unsaid? Please write soon. I miss you (and your letters).

love, david

So, there it was. As she had written in her inscription in the Tanakh that she sent me: "Cast your bread on the waters, for in the fullness of days you will find it." After eight months of intellectual and ideological musings and a lot of joking around, I finally put on paper what had been brewing in my head, at least since Racheli's visit in February and, likely, long before that. Now, I had to wait for her reply.

MAY 11, 1971: RACHELI

David's letter of May 3 threw open the invisible gates holding back a conversation about our relationship. I immediately responded:

It's so much easier now. I've read your letter many times – between

the lines, yours or mine. It's so much better now. But it's harder
too. That is good. It's like the difference between fingering the forms
of glassware covered with a piece of cloth – you are very careful,
you can feel the shapes but you can't see through; you don't know
where to be careful – and then you may hit hard without knowing
it. And when you've taken off the cover – and the very fine glass
shines – you realize how uncareful you actually have been, and
you touch each piece so very lightly, gently.

I echoed David's questioning: "Where is this going from here?" and
said: "I've asked myself that maybe too often. Asking hasn't led me
anywhere. Whatever <u>was</u> there developed because I was constantly
conscious of this 'where to?'" I encouraged David – and myself –
to allow this uncertainty, to be patient. I translated this into the
practicalities of what we were planning for the next year of our lives.
David would stay in Berkeley to go to graduate school and I would
go into the army. We would have to wait a long time to see "where
this is going."

Suddenly, my perspective shifted: it was good that I would be
going into the army. It would be easier to tolerate the wait because
I would have no choice, because my brain would be filled with what
I expected would be essential and, yet, totally useless information:
how to take apart a Czech-made rifle left over from the 1948 war,
how to march in orderly triplets, how many millimeters between
your stretched fingers and eyebrow make for the perfect salute.
It would make the time pass faster until we really had to face the
momentous decision about our relationship and life trajectories. I
tried to cheer us up and on with the Beatles: "The two of us writing
letters, sending postcards – on our way back home. You and I have
memories... a road that stretches out ahead."

MAY 19, 1971: DAVID

Racheli's quite wonderful response to my letter that "broke the
ice," or, as she put it much more poetically, that removed the cloth

covering the piece of glass we were both trying to touch, seemed to open a new level of honesty and self-reflection. Now, the persona I had constructed in my letters had to give way to my true, inner self. I confessed that, despite the appearance that I might convey, "I cover my feelings with concealing layers of words and activities so that the rich silence inside seems irretrievably hidden." I had just read Hayim Nachman Bialik's essay "Revelation and Concealment in Language," which is all about how words conceal the truth. Only poetry, says Bialik, can use words the way music uses notes, to really communicate. But, despite occasional attempts to write poetry, I was not really a poet.

I asked Racheli to always be critical of me and not only to be honest about herself. In that vein, I took exception to her statement in her letter that she found me "too brilliant:"

> *That is something I've always thought about you. I guess that neither of us is really as smart as the other one thinks, and more important are the faults which such one-sided impressions cover up. Acting smart is always a good way to conceal the lonely, uncertain person you are inside.*
>
> *The best thing for me is to break holes in my protective shell, but I have trouble doing it. Why? Because my biggest fault is that I am self-centered and selfish. I guess I don't tell many people that, but I want you to know it. And I'm also afraid to try anything new that might disturb the secure world I've created for myself.*

Committing to this relationship would certainly challenge this "secure world." We were both now about to embark on two separate paths. Would these entirely different worlds change us so that we would no longer find ourselves on the same wavelength? Little did I know how much our relationship would be put to the test in the many months to come.

MAY 24, 1971: RACHELI

Our letters were much more serious and emotionally intense

now. I tried to reassure David that the fact that every decision and communication felt fraught was fine, but it was myself I was trying just as hard to reassure.

Another whole year and no hope for a U.J.A mission, maybe even more? We seem to sound somehow so helpless, in pain, and your letters don't exactly make me happy anymore. Writing to you doesn't either, it confuses me.

I put the pen down – it was too much. I continued the next morning: "I stopped writing last night because I sounded too desperate; I was." I concluded with what quickly became a constant refrain: "Could you, please, write soon so that I don't feel that much the 10,000 miles the letter has to travel to reach you." But even though I appealed to David to write me as often as possible, I didn't hold up my end of the bargain. I went silent for nearly a month.

MAY 30, 1971: DAVID

I think that the last thing I anticipated was that a mutual affirmation of our feelings for each other would make us unhappy. Racheli thought that the letters made both of us feel rather helpless, and, then, paradoxically, she asked me to write as often as possible. Could letters expressing the distance between us also bridge that gap? I felt the same confusion she did and confessed to spending ten minutes thinking about what to write from one sentence to the next. While Racheli's future – or, at least, the next couple of years – was already more or less set in stone by the army, my own was still up in the air.

Even though I'd written before about my doubts, I now felt it possible to speak about them more openly:

I definitely want to study more but I'm having my usual doubts about what to do with it. If I get a PhD in this country and decide to stay here, I will probably end up at some crummy little college in some obscure corner of America. That is absolutely the last thing I would settle for. The pull to come to Israel is strong – I don't have to tell you that. I think I could be comfortable living in Berkeley for the rest of my life, but somehow it doesn't seem serious enough, a cop-out. Maybe the solution is to organize my hevre to make aliya. There is already talk of forming a garin [a group planning to join a kibbutz]. But if I do want to do serious graduate work, then I think I have to do part of it here.

Little could I have known that this paragraph already foretold the various way-stations of my life. Our group did form a *garin*, which went to Kibbutz Gezer. But we dropped out before that as I became more engrossed in my dissertation. In fact, it was during a four-month research stint in Jerusalem in 1975 when I decided that I wanted an academic career rather than life on a kibbutz. And that career did, indeed, start in an obscure corner of America: Binghamton, New York (the university, however, was not so "crummy"). Nine years later, a job offer brought us back to Berkeley, where, as my letter prophesies, I have been happily living out the rest of my life.

All that lay in the future. For now, I was kicking myself. I had been offered a number of possibilities to come to Israel that summer for free, but I had already accepted a job as program director at a Young Judaea Camp in the wine country of the Napa Valley. Too bad that I was so slow writing that May 3 letter! If I had broken the ice earlier, we would have had a chance to see whether this epistolary relationship had any legs in reality.

JUNE 3 – JUNE 21, 1971: DAVID

By early June, I was able to report that I had finished thirty pages of my Berdichevsky study and it threatened to turn into a book. Webster, that "cranky, old eccentric professor who was grading it," had read the first chapter and, to my astonishment: "HE LIKED IT." I was set to graduate in a week and half, but it didn't look like I would be done by then. In fact, I submitted a rough draft, which was judged sufficient for "high honors," but not "highest honors," which the head of the program told me I would have gotten if I had submitted a polished version. Ah, well! It turned out to have made no difference in terms of my academic future.

There was one striking moment in the graduation ceremony. I was the only student working on a theme in Jewish history in the department. During the reception afterwards, a distinguished medievalist, Gerald Caspari, who I'm not sure anyone knew to be Jewish, came up to me and, evidently moved by the fact that a student showed some interest in the history of the Jews, told me the following story. He was a child in Paris during World War II, when the French police came to take the family away. They asked how many children there were and his mother answered: "one." And, so, he was saved and his brother was not.

After the graduation, Professor Webster showed a hitherto unknown side of his personality: generosity. His practice had been to invite students for lunch and then make them pay their share. Now, he treated me and my parents to a sumptuous Chinese meal and then invited us to his house for dessert. There, he regaled us with his theories about the end of the world. My mother and I listened politely, but my father reacted in a way that probably no one had ever done before: he fell asleep! The next day, Webster told me that my father was a nasty person but that my mother was very nice.

Working with Webster had been a disorienting experience. It was intellectually exciting, of course, but as I wrote to Racheli:

> *He himself wonders whether doing history is of any use and he hates the academic community. But, on the other hand, he is so wrapped up in intellectual games that he has lost the ability to relate to people on any other level. He scares me because I can see myself ending up like him (not exactly – he is really crazy and I am not -- yet).*

As I learned much later, he also lived a secret life as a gay man, visiting the bath houses in San Francisco before anyone knew about AIDS, from which he died around the year 2000. He had wanted to live in Israel, but after a year's sabbatical there, "he couldn't stand it.

Now, he lives in a kind of limbo, waiting for the Messiah, which is
hard for him, because he's a skeptic." Could I somehow reconcile my
desires to lead an intellectually satisfying life while also realizing my
ideals without succumbing to Webster's conundrum?

I confessed that my intellectual and emotional ambivalences were
what drew me to Berdichevsky, who was famously torn between the
world of his birth and the new world he wanted to create. I had sent
my paper to Racheli and now warned her: "Read carefully. I think
that there is a lot of myself in that paper."

David's graduation: with his father, Jacob, and Prof. Richard Webster

JUNE 19, 1971: RACHELI

Nearly four weeks went by before I finally wrote again: "I am
very sorry, almost feel guilty, for not having written. I needed time to
adjust – all this is going so fast – you graduating, and more than that,
deciding finally not to come here." I had known for a while that this
was coming – David's graduation, his decision to stay in Berkeley,

and the resulting long separation while I was in the army and he in graduate school -- but I still needed time, and evidently a hiatus in letter-writing, to sort it out in my head and my heart. I felt perhaps more acutely than David that our relationship was hobbled by the huge gaps between the realities of our lives. I felt I needed to explain myself: "our relationship is not a part of my life. It's a heavy and dear part of my mind, but it's disconnected from, even alien, to what I do and how I live." At the same time, I felt that since my emotional and intellectual life was taking place in our letters, my daily life and work seemed hollow. And I already anticipated this sort-of-schizophrenia would increase many-fold when I started my army service.

What we needed, I told David, were ways to make our relationship more "real" and avenues for being more engaged in each other's lives. I expressed my wish to be more hooked into his passions and preoccupations with my typical chutzpa: a request for the Jewish Radical to have an issue devoted to what I was deeply concerned with.

I would like to see an issue of the J.R. devoted to the problem of Diaspora and Israel as a personal dilemma, to see how "Radical Jews" deal with it, with Rosenzweig, Borochov, and America today, Israel today, and so on.

And lo and behold, they did! The Fall 1971 issue was on that theme and included an essay by me, refashioned from a letter I would write to David on July 17.

JUNE 24, 1971: DAVID

I suddenly fell upon a solution to our conundrum and sent it via special delivery: "Dearest Racheli, what if I came to Israel for four weeks at the end of August until the end of September? When do you go in the army?"

To this I appended a passage from Elie Wiesel's *Town Beyond the Wall* (I was still in my Wiesel phase):

It's the divine will that when a man has something to say, he says it most perfectly by taking unto him a woman and creating a new man. And then God remembers that he too has something to say and he entrusts it to the Angel of Death. But even so, your creation is not a total loss. Something of it persists ... Man may not have the last word, but he has the last cry. That moment marks the birth of art.

A real relationship -- "when a man has something to say" -- I wrote, requires touching and not only writing.

JUNE 25, 1971: DAVID

Inspired by my plan to come to Israel at the end of the summer, I now wrote almost every day or every other day. On Friday evening, I sent what was probably my most "religious" letter of all our correspondence:

It seems to me that I could not establish a home and bring up a family without some increased commitment to halacha – perhaps only in observance of Shabbat in some fashion. I am for the first time in my life beginning to understand what it might mean to pray in a really Jewish way. To have Shabbat dinner with friends, sing zemirot far into the night, study together, exchange midrashim. It is particularly amazing that the same passage from Psalms hit us both at the same time. While I've been singing the Shir ha-Ma'alot [the Psalm that begins the prayer after meals] for many years, for the first time, I looked at the words and realized how incomparably great they are:

Return us, O God, like flash floods in the desert
He who sows in sorrow, will reap in joy

A Nobel Prize to the guy who wrote that!

JUNE 27, 1971: DAVID

And, then, I more or less contradicted myself. The camp where I was to serve as program director was under the auspices of Young

Judaea. In July 1967, right after the Six Day War, I had taken a summer job as a counselor with a camp from the same movement in Southern California, even though I had never even heard of it before, much less belonged to it. When that camp was over at the end of July, they needed counselors for their Northern California camp. I had made some wonderful friends and they turned to me now, four years later, to join them again, this time in the wine country of the Napa Valley.

However, even before the camp began, I got into ferocious arguments with the camp leadership. Young Judaea was an ecumenical Zionist movement that belonged to none of the Zionist political parties. I took issue with their "liberal" model: "They want to present all viewpoints and not make a conscious choice and ideological decision." I thought that this was a wrongheaded educational approach. The kids ought to be given a definite direction, which, overheated ideologue that I was, I thought should be socialist and Zionist. I was going to have a problem teaching things I didn't believe in. And I had a problem with their religious orientation:

> *The camp actually does have a viewpoint, even if they won't admit it. They want to give the kids a dose of real Orthodox Judaism. For example, they insist on observing Shabbat as much as possible, down to not cooking hot food. All this is fine if you believe in it, but it's hard for me to accept and to explain to the kids. I can see the value in observance of Shabbat, but I'm against defining Judaism as merely the observance of mitzvot.*

I was also charged with leading Shabbat morning prayers because nobody else wanted to do it:

> *It's absurd, of course, because I have no idea how to do these things since I almost never go to synagogue. This will be what is called "creative services" – any resemblance to the traditional will be purely coincidental (from now on, you can call me Reb David)."*

Then, climbing down from my ideological tree, I returned to the personal. Two of my close comrades from Berkeley, Sherman Rosenfeld and Marcie Lincoff, were going to Israel for the summer and I deputized

Racheli at Belvoir

both them to look up Racheli. In addition to informing her of their imminent arrival, I also made the following request: "Do you have a good picture of yourself to send me? These letters are not very graphic." She didn't, but Marcie took one at Belvoir, the Crusader castle overlooking the Jordan Valley. It became my favorite picture of Racheli, since it seemed to capture so much of her spirit.

JUNE 29, 1971: RACHELI

That special delivery letter, sent June 24, traversed the huge geographical space between us unusually fast and I received it on June 29th. I was giddy when David broke our tortured impasse by suggesting he would come to Israel at the end of August. Between the end of his summer camp counselor duties and my draft into the IDF we could carve out a mini "Summer of Love," finally be together and road-test our budding romance. I responded with a poem by Rachel, the beloved Israeli poet whose loves were all frustrated and unrequited.

> Can you hear my voice, my far-away one?
> Can you hear my voice, wherever you are?
> A voice calling out loud
> A voice calling out in silence
> And transcending time, grants a blessing.
>
> This universe is vast
> With many paths,

Meeting momentarily
Sundering apart for eternity.

For some reason I did not include the two, concluding lines: "I shall wait for you till the last of my days, as [the biblical matriarch] Rachel had waited for her beloved." Was I leery of promising to wait to my last day? Was the triple Rachel -- my name, the poet's, and the biblical matriarch -- just too melodramatic? After all, both those Rachels were tragic figures. The poet died alone at a young age and the biblical Rachel died in childbirth, becoming the personification of maternal grief: "a keening and bitter cry, Rachel weeps over her sons, refuses to be consoled" (Jeremiah 31:14).

But I hastened to balance the dark poem with hopefulness: "not 'Sundering apart for eternity,'" I assured David. And regarding our anxiety about "What will happen if you come to Israel?" I was cautious but optimistic: "It's too hard to answer. A lot, I think, - no, I <u>feel</u>. Because the answers, finally, are emotional, not philosophical."

And, quickly, I veered towards the practicalities: "here are the facts you need to know: I'll be going into the Army around Sept. 20th – I'm not sure yet. I'll find out as soon as possible. I'll be more or less free then, from the second week of August till I get drafted."

JULY 2, 1971: RACHELI

In late June, as David had already promised, I had a transfusion of "Berkeley vibes" via his close friends who were in Israel for extended stays:

It was so good to be together and there was so much of <u>you</u> in this. It is a strong connection. But when they all left, I suddenly felt, maybe this time more than I ever did, how much I miss you. Maybe I feel strangely because you seemed so close – all these people projecting "you," and at the same time so far.

As of this writing, I still wasn't absolutely sure that David would be coming in August. It seemed too good to be true and my draft date was

still unconfirmed. It would mean the difference between "a high point
- at those moments that I get carried away by the hope that you'll come
and a "deep hole," that you won't be able to come." As was my wont, I
turned to poetry, this time quoting a beloved Leah Goldberg poem:

> If you give me my part in the fright of your darkness
> Perhaps a small light will shine for me.
> If you unburden onto my shoulder the heavy weight from yours
> Perhaps it will be a little lighter for me.
> If you bring into the frost of my abandonment the cold of your
> loneliness
> Perhaps it will be a bit warmer for me
>
> Like a tree in its snows that harbors the shoots of spring
> In the frost
> I will stand at the door of your sadness.
> And your pain shall be a gift to me
> In good hands I will carry it
> I will not fall; I will not kneel
> Don't be afraid.

I couldn't have said it better: the burdens we carried seemed so
uneven. David was agonizing about both his short-term plans and
his long-term future, while I walked the easy path of certainty: I had
to go into the army for the next two years and my future was on a
kibbutz, probably my own Kfar Ruppin.

JULY 12, 1971: DAVID

Before the start of camp, I went down to Los Angeles and embarked
on a four-day backpacking trip in the Kings Canyon region of the Sierra
Nevada mountains. I went with my father, sister Lorah, and David
Berner, one of the two Hillel rabbis at UCLA, who later moved to Israel:

Despite clouds of mosquitoes, it was very beautiful – lots of water

crashing down on all sides (the water in the Sierra's makes you drunk
after one cupful, but just to be sure, we took along some brandy). On
Erev Shabbat, we said Kiddush and sang Shalom Aleichem.

I returned to Berkeley to meet one of my fellow counselors, Noam
Sachs (later Zion), a graduate student in philosophy at Columbia
University, who became a life-long friend. I had never met anyone
quite like Noam: a fairly Orthodox Jew with a deep philosophical
education, pedagogical creativity, an irreverent spirit, and "a radical
Zionist of my type and, from that point of view, we have a lot in
common." He stayed with me for a week until the camp started,
during which time, in what would become a running joke between
us for the next fifty years, he would wake me up every morning by
sitting on my feet and provoking a philosophical debate. When the
1973 Yom Kippur War broke out, Noam abandoned his graduate
program and moved to Israel where he became one of the foremost
pedagogues at the Shalom Hartman Institute in Jerusalem.

Once the camp began, I confronted a bit of a pedagogical challenge
myself, since, as the program director, I was supposed to serve as
a resource for the other counselors. Could I muster up sufficient
creativity? As I wrote to Racheli, whose gift with children I had already
noticed the previous summer and who would go on in later years to
a career (among many other things) as an educator and parenting
counselor: "The more education, the less creativity, I think. But in order
to educate kids, one has to think the way they do, which always amazes
me. Maybe I'll experience a return to childhood and get original."

And, then, to the most important part of the letter: "August 30,
5:35 pm (BOAC Flight 314)." I had already sent that information in
early July on a postcard with a picture of a waterfall from the Sierras.
Now that I had actually bought my ticket, our relationship no longer
seemed like a romantic dream, but instead like a concrete reality:

Now comes the real test: will we be closer in letters (in fantasies
and dreams) than in actuality – in talking and touching and
being with each other with real hopes and desires and also

problems? I feel funny writing you the date, as if it is a step off a
cliff over an abyss that I can't see very well. I also think (I probably
shouldn't) of another date, three weeks after this one. If the answer
to my question is "yes," will I want to leave? And if the answer is
"no," will I feel as if I made a mistake? But all this is an idiotic
intellectual game like we learn at school where we try to foresee
all alternatives and never listen to the small, still voice that comes
from some place deeper than the brain.

JULY 12, 1971: RACHELI

The uncertainty about David's visit had been exhausting, but
it ended when I got his postcard announcing an arrival date, time,
and flight number! I was ecstatic and also terrified, as was David, of
plunging into the unknown: "I guess we are both (and have been)
scared of what's going to happen to us when we step into something
new, when there's a change in our relationship. . . maybe afraid of
losing each other, ourselves." But I was mostly optimistic, I knew
there was something real and deep that held us together. It was just
the maneuvering from an epistolary relationship, where paper, ink
and time separated us and allowed each of us to frame our thoughts
ever so carefully, to being together in the flesh and blood. It made
me wonder about the aborted feeling we were left with after my visit
in February: "Is this why it took us so long to open up in our letters,
why we felt some awkwardness when I was there, when the situation
changed from writing our letters that were easy to handle?"

I had to fill the time between that moment and David's arrival
which, in my mind, was already unrolling like a spool inadvertently
dropped from shaking hands. I reported on my incredibly busy day-
to-day life, at that moment in such stark contrast to my fantasies about
our soon-to-be time together. We were in similar circumstances,
both of us working as summer camp counselors:

Now that I'm on a Work Camp and I live with the kids, I have
to be so involved with all these things – it's a serious case of split

personality. I have to be everyone's 1. Mother; 2. Counselor; 3. Metapelet [Child Caretaker]; 4. Work assignment manager; 5. Mailman; 6. Telephone; 7. Nurse; 8. Babysitter. . . very tiring. I find that I just have to get away from the kids for at least an hour a day for "soul-resting" and I find it hard to cover up my feelings when they get on my nerves. You probably have the same thing with your kids at camp.

I went on to complain about how lazy and inconsiderate the kids were, comparing them unfavorably to kibbutz kids who "know how to work" and how to sleep in the same room with their peers without keeping everyone awake half the night. But I, too, hardly slept: "I'm waiting -- 'I am asleep but my heart is awake.'"

JULY 17, 1971: RACHELI

In response to David's ideological differences with the Young Judaea summer camp, I questioned the value of the whole enterprise:

I think the work you are doing is very important but it seems to me there is a very big question as to its significance and future in America. I don't know how you feel about this, but I'm worried because America today seems so mixed up, with a great potential for a violent outburst of revolution, which will cause a lot of destruction, insecurity, socially and ideologically, disorientation and a certain blindness to truth.

This was America as seen by an outsider in 1971, probably reflecting what I had experienced in Boston in 1968, especially the assassinations of Martin Luther King Jr. and Bobby Kennedy, and the reports I followed assiduously about the protests against the Vietnam War and the riots at the Democratic Convention. But it seems now, as I write, alarmingly relevant to our own times.

And, while I was still prone to striking a patriotic, pro-Israel pose, I wasn't any more optimistic about its state of affairs, neither present nor future:

*I'm afraid Israel is going towards mis-orientation, losing truth,
too, not because of a violent mixture of revolution, but the
opposite – a certain apathy, neglect of ideology and ideologically-
motivated thought and action, because of our tendency to settle
down, for individual peace and comfort. It's easy to understand
and it's hard to change people who fought most of their lives for
a national and an individual independence, security and well-
being, becoming bourgeois, non-Zionist, negating the revolution
they themselves created, fought for, lived for, and returning to their
parents' way of life.*

But it was not just ideological theorizing: behind my critique of
Israeli society was hidden, and not too well, my desire to convince
David to come to Israel. In a kind of manifesto over many sloppily-
written pages, I tried to make an argument for why living in Israel
is essential to a vibrant, authentic Jewish identity. I attempted to
harmonize the thoughts of our heroes, Rosenzweig (who was a non-
Zionist) and A.D. Gordon (the prophet of the Zionist "religion of
labor"), while admitting I couldn't quite make the twain meet in a
way that felt genuine either to my experience, or to their theology:

*We need a synthesis of Rosenzweig's Judaism with Gordon.
Rosenzweig doesn't fully realize, I think, the meaning and
implications of the return to Israel, the establishment of a new,
renewed bond with the homeland. For Rosenzweig the culturally-
rich existence of Diaspora will assure that bond with Israel. But
what about the people here who need to combine this emotional,
ideological, abstract bond to Israel with a real bond living here,
working the land? This is one of the major problems for Gordon -
emotionally experiencing being a stranger in his homeland.*

I went on and on about the dilemma of creating a Jewish identity that
fused those two thinkers. But I was stuck and, perhaps presciently,
realized that philosophy and ideology would not, ultimately, provide
an answer. I needed to draw my answers from life: "Maybe I need

to go through a major change – emotionally, objectively - to be able to see myself differently." Which brought me right back to the huge change I was anticipating: David's visit.

I was so excited about his arrival that I relegated a potential problem to a P.S., at the very end of this long letter:

> *I went to find out about getting drafted – not such good news. I'll get my exact date next week or so, but it'll probably be as soon as the middle of Sept. I hope it's later but, maybe not. Is there any possibility for you to make it here earlier? I don't think there's any way, any possibility of delaying the date of my draft.*

As if scared by my own words, I quickly turned back to hopefulness: "I can't wait for that complete relief, whole and peaceful, when I see you, when I hug you, when you are here. I'm afraid I could cry. I miss you so much I can't wait any longer."

END OF JULY (UNDATED), 1971: DAVID

I was back in Berkeley for a three-day break between the July and August sessions of the camp. I spoke to two of my professors about possibly staying in Israel for the coming year to do some graduate level courses. They strongly advised me to do an MA in Berkeley first and go to Israel afterwards, especially since Berkeley was giving me a fellowship. I was not so certain that this was what I wanted to do, but I accepted their advice.

As to the camp, I reported a mixed reaction to my role there. Some of the other counselors were lukewarm about my ideas, but I also had some successes: "I gave a *sicha* [discussion] for the oldest kids on a radical critique of the American Jewish community. Afterwards, all the best kids wanted to sign up for the Radical Jewish Union." I also designed a program on the Holocaust. I had chosen various songs and a reading of *Nightwords*, an amazing liturgy of texts from Jewish and non-Jewish sources assembled by the Yiddish scholar, David Roskies, while he was still a graduate student (I still think that this is one of the best things ever composed in response to the Holocaust). The campers walked to the campfire area in the dark, with candles lighting the way. It turned out that the program had a profound effect on the kids, particularly a few older girls who became very upset. One had never even heard of the six million. I was impressed by how the two Israelis in the camp (a 17-year-old Scout and a 15-year-old camper) were the most effective in calming those who were most upset. This led me to following observation:

There must be something in the Israeli experience that conditions everyone to dealing with tragedy. American kids rarely have that kind of strength. Without it, people live much more shallow lives; perhaps they never really mature. That strength that comes from tragedy is also typically Jewish (are Jews therefore a mature people?). Perhaps that is why it is hard for American Jews to remain authentically Jewish.

David and Tom on the steps of Sproul Hall, Berkeley Campus

The subject of tragedy led to an unrelated topic. During the three-day weekend, I stayed back in Berkeley with my dear friend and roommate, Tom Stehling, who was a music aficionado. So, I took advantage of Tom's remarkable record collection (Tom came out as gay when we lived together and was later the first person I knew to die of AIDS).

Speaking of tragedy: just finished listening to Beethoven's "Pathétique" Sonata. Ah, Beethoven, you had a Jewish soul! Must put on some Mozart and Bach (Ah, Mozart!

Ah, Bach!). Do you know the story? When God sits on his throne in all his glory, he listens to Bach. But when he just wants to have fun, he listens to Mozart.

Decades later, when I took up piano as an adult, I actually succeeded in playing the "Pathétique." Although the quality of my playing certainly left a lot to be desired, immersing myself in it made me realize even more its profundity.

I had just finished reading Amos Elon's wonderful book *The Israelis: Founders and Sons* and recommended it enthusiastically to Racheli. I thought it was perhaps the finest thing I had read on the history of Israel:

The curious thing is that I belong ideologically more to the generation of the founders than to the sons. But is that also true of young Israelis like you who are becoming interested in Gordon, Rosenzweig and the tradition generally? I hope so.

However, I had to confess that my relationship to Israel was no longer either objective or ideological: "My primary feelings are wrapped up with you."

AUGUST 5, 1971: DAVID

Just as I was anticipating an imminent reunion with Racheli, disaster struck. I'm not sure if the news came via a telegram she sent to my parents or a phone call, because there is nothing in our letters. However, it becomes clear from what I wrote on August 5: "This is going to be a very difficult letter. Yesterday, I canceled my ticket. I'm not coming. I feel disoriented, like my feet can't find firm ground."

What had happened? The army had moved up her draft date by two weeks to around September 7, so we would have had no more than a week together. I continued in despair:

I am afraid of losing you, afraid because next year seems so empty, the future so empty. A year seems forever – it is bad having a year ahead of you that you wish was over. Why did I want to

come to Israel at all? To find out if I'm in love with you. A week
is too short, impossible. I can't write anymore. Please write soon,
Racheli my love.

AUGUST 13, 1971: DAVID

August 13 was Racheli's birthday. I sent her a celebratory, if
cryptic telegram from St. Helena, California, where the camp was
located: "Happy Chai plus one [i.e., 18+1]. Shir Ha-Shirim 2:14." That
verse reads: "My dove is in the cleft of the rock, in the secret recesses
of the cliff. Let me see your face, let me hear your voice, for your
voice is sweet and your face is lovely." And, then, in a letter written
the same day in Hebrew:

It is again Shabbat and a time when the joy is yet mingled with
sadness because I miss you. It is a sadness that, somehow, we must
learn to live with for a while. We must not allow it to consume
us, for then we would try to get rid of it by forgetting each other.
"The ones who sow in tears, shall reap in gladness" [Psalms 126:5]:
It is your birthday today. One year older. But we remain the
same distance apart (both in time, age, and space) – at least the
distance is not growing and it will someday soon be so close as to
be unnoticeable. Sometimes I feel very, very strongly that "I am
in exile" – like Berdichevsky, a personal exile, as well as part of
"my people's exile."

In a postscript response to her earlier question why I had called her
"Rachel," I explained: "I was calling you 'Rachel' because 'Racheli' seems
like a little girl's name (which you aren't anymore, Old Lady) and also
because I feel like calling you something you aren't normally called."

AUGUST 17, 1971: DAVID

Since it looked like we were going to have to return to the old-
fashioned epistolary way of keeping our love alive, I composed a
description about what I did when I received a letter:

Reactions on receiving a letter from you: at first, when I see your letter in the box, even though I rush (as I do every morning) to see if there is anything from you, I have to rip myself away from the partial reality of everything that's going on around here and let my other personality (frozen in boxes and bags of the US and Israeli Post Offices) come out. Feelings of depression because I know that once I finish reading the letter, I would feel sad because there is no more to read and the only thing there is to do is to pull myself to my typewriter and start another letter. I put your letter in my pocket, trying to postpone reading it, trying to draw out the expectation, excitement and uncertainty that always comes with receiving a letter. Finally, I can't stand it anymore. I go to my room, open the envelope and pull one sheet out. Then, much to my surprise, I read the letter and feel very happy, as if my lagging spirits were boosted by just that slight contact with you.

AUGUST 22, 1971: RACHELI

I fell into a long silence, even as David was pleading for more letters from me. I finally wrote:

I found myself somehow in need of a longer break after our last letters. I didn't want to sound as sad as I was and couldn't write without getting to that. Yes, I must learn to enjoy myself without letting myself stop at that moment when your absence enters my mind.

I then tried to enumerate some of my activities in the effort to keep myself going and happy: my farewell visit to the Communa, reflecting, yet again, on "how much I love these people" and learning to play the guitar, which never went very far. I doubt that any of it helped much, but perhaps what did was the fact that I was about to start a totally different chapter in my life, one where I felt my "self" was going to be put into the deep freeze: my service in the army.

I did not worry much about the army service as far as physical challenges and the discomfort of life on an army base. I felt that, as a kibbutznik, I was certainly tough enough to handle any rigors the army threw my way. And, having already been away from home for a year, I also had no worries about what is hardest for most new recruits: being far from Mom and Dad. Rather, I dreaded losing my intellectual identity and emotional life, including, of course, the intense connection with David:

> I somehow fear that these years in the army are going to cut me off from something that might be the source of my development, as it requires having "mental free space." And the first thing they do in the army is get hold of your private space and time, so as to change you from a person to a soldier.

That didn't actually happen. On the contrary, it was the letters – writing them and reading them – that kept my private mental space intact during my service.

I also had fantasies about using my army service as a vehicle for continuing to explore the Jewish identity question. So, even before being drafted, I wrote David about my "brilliant plan:"

> I've been thinking of trying to get to be an NCO in a religious army settlement (he'achzut). Being in a religious one means experiencing life with complete adherence to the mitzvot but:
> 1. For a limited amount of time with no obligations-an experiment.
> 2. Some of the objective difficulties taken off, as it's in a kibbutz.
> 3. Being with young people who themselves are questioning and seeking answers for a way of life. . . and are relatively (compared to what we find in other Jewish circles in Israel) very open-minded "Bnei Akiva" [members of the Religious Youth Movement].

The plan did not materialize. Despite intensive efforts, I was stationed in a secular he'achzut, overlooking the Dead Sea, to which I will return in due course.

I anticipated that once I was drafted, I would have to switch from English to Hebrew since my letters would go through military censorship: "Imagine – you're not the only one who's going to read my letters. Strange. Maybe I should add something in each letter for

Yossarian, too," a reference to *Catch-22* where Yossarian hilariously – and subversively - censors the letters of the enlisted men while lying in the hospital. In the end, though, I was able to write from the army in English, although I reserved Hebrew for especially emotional letters.

AUGUST 24, 1971: DAVID

After the conclusion of the camp, Noam Sachs and I went to San Francisco where he was intent on experiencing Shlomo Carlebach's famous House of Love and Prayer. I had an allergic reaction:

These people are very passive, abstract and mystical types with little solid rooting in serious study. Everybody must love everybody else. Yech – too much mush! I like cynical, funny, articulate, hard-headed, aggressive, intelligent Jews – not these birds. Unfortunately, this trend towards passive, mystical, anti-intellectual behavior ("everything in life is beautiful") has become sanctified as the "counterculture." Well - I don't like this "culture" or the "counterculture." Where does that leave me? In Exile.

Once the interminable Friday evening Shabbat service was over (around 11:00 pm!), Noam and I retreated to the vacant apartment where we were staying. The next day, instead of returning to the House of Love of Prayer, we studied Tanakh: Second Isaiah, a chapter from Deuteronomy and some Songs of Exultation from Psalms. I had a kind of epiphany: "It was very exciting – I must study Bible!!!!!!! (Will you teach me?). One of the only real ways to become a complete Jew is through the Bible." Study, not prayer, was fast becoming the core and compass of my Jewish identity.

AUGUST 28, 1971: DAVID

I hopped over from San Francisco to Berkeley to try to find an apartment for the coming year. I called listing after listing, with no luck. Finally, with the very last number, I struck gold: a beautiful, large room in a charming Victorian house on a one-block street on the southside of the Berkeley campus. Just before departing for the airport to fly to Los Angeles, my father called to say that he had received a telegram from Racheli that the Israeli army had moved her draft date back to September 19! Our wheel of fortune had turned again, but I had already sold my ticket and it was too late to get another at the last minute. "This whole plan really turned into a *balagan* [mess]," I wrote.

AUGUST 30, 1971: RACHELI

Somehow, I managed to bounce back from the crushing disappointment more easily than I would have thought, perhaps because at the time I was home on the kibbutz working, getting up at 5:00 am every morning for the olive harvest and trying to cram into my free time all the things I still wanted to do before being drafted. David and I managed to connect by phone on August 30, after he had gotten to Los Angeles. Our phone call, short as it was, made the distance seem tolerable: "It's strange – we just talked today – it somehow seemed natural. It felt like we were both here – in a bus-ride's distance."

In the two weeks before my draft date, I spent a lot of time thinking. In fact, I cherished "the first Shabbat Eve I have for myself in a year, the first one that is not filled with other people. The first Shabbat Eve I'm alone, thinking a lot about Shabbat - for the future and in the present." I made a real effort to feel the presence of Shabbat, which was hard on my kibbutz, where Shabbat was totally secularized. It was simply a day of rest with minimal vestiges of the traditional rituals, so, I didn't actually perform any: it was all in my head. But I had a deep insight:

> *Right now, I discovered a certain notion in me – that lighting the candles (I guess especially that as opposed to singing, studying Torah, and maybe also because I know it is my role as a woman, somewhere in the darkness of a subconscious "Jewish perception" of myself) won't make sense to me until I have established a home – until I have my children watch the candles with me.*

But that, I acknowledged, was in the distant future: "Now, the

Shabbat seems to be filled with more emptiness than holiness." Yet
it was not, actually, altogether empty for me:

> *It's close to Kabbalat Shabbat now, and you can read in the Siddur
> in small print: 'On Shabbat Eve, before welcoming the Shabbat,
> you recite the Song of Songs with melodies.' Please do. Shabbat
> shalom. I miss you more on Shabbat night.*

AUGUST 30, 1971: DAVID

Racheli's call had woken me up early in the morning, Los Angeles
time, but I didn't mind. I wrote:

> *In spite of my incoherent state of mind, I was really happy to hear
> your voice. It suddenly hit me in a flash as I was talking to you
> how difficult it is to have to go into the army for 20 months. Of
> course, you were saying it in your letters for months, but I never
> really paid proper attention. I suddenly realized how I would feel
> knowing that in a few weeks I would have no control of my life,
> never given a moment's privacy and subjected to the most idiotic
> sorts of activities (no matter how people rationalize it, being a
> soldier remains the most antithetical to being human).*

I was obviously projecting onto the Israeli army my own feelings
about the American army, in whose clutches I feared that I might
find myself in the near future.

I allowed that, once basic training was over, Racheli might find
a more humane way to serve and I approved of her idea of joining
a religious Nachal settlement: "I'm very proud of you. I don't know
many Israelis (or American Jews, for that matter) who are open-
minded or brave enough to look honestly at the Jewish tradition and
try something, which is, at first, very foreign."

SEPTEMBER 4, 1971: DAVID

While in Los Angeles, I paid a visit to Rabbi Moshe Adler, who had so impressed me on a previous visit. We talked about how an Orthodox Jew dealt with the Holocaust. He thought that the suffering servant of Isaiah 53, so beloved of Christians as a prefiguration of Jesus, might provide a possible answer: the people of Israel were God's suffering servants. I couldn't accept this idea because it might imply that the Holocaust was an expiation for sins, and because then the perpetrators would be somehow relieved of their moral responsibility for evil.

Moshe also spoke of the idea that there are many "handles" to the Torah and that each person has his or her own handle. For some, it might be Shabbat, for others a life of mitzvot. Still in the afterglow of my intensive study session with Noam in San Francisco, I said that my handle must be study without adherence to Jewish law. But would study lead me to a life of faith or on a path of rejection? Neither, to judge by how my life has unfolded: the secular study of Jewish sources would serve for me as *talmud torah,* the study of Torah, traditionally considered equal to fulfilling all the commandments.

Moshe and I studied the texts about the two messiahs: Messiah son of Joseph and Messiah son of David. The first was supposed to be a warrior messiah, who would die in battle, to be succeeded by the Messiah son of David, who would usher in world peace. Moshe cited his teacher, who had explained this as follows: the first messiah will take the Jews out of the Galut, while the second will take the Galut out of the Jews. This rather appealed to me.

Although I was despondent to be in Los Angeles for the next month rather than in Israel, it turned into a rather momentous visit in terms of my future. I had heard from my father about a brilliant young Jewish historian, Amos Funkenstein, who had come to UCLA four years earlier. With little to occupy me, I decided to audit Professor Funkenstein's summer school lectures on Second Temple and Hellenistic Jewish history. I was blown away! Here was an intellect the like of which I had never encountered. To be in his presence was to watch a spectacular mind thinking. We struck up a conversation in his office and I showed him my Berdichevsky paper. He not only liked it but also suggested expanding it into a doctoral dissertation on "Radical Jewish Counter-Histories." Six years later, that is, more or less, what happened, with Funkenstein as my advisor.

SEPTEMBER 9, 1971: RACHELI

As David and I pivoted back to a letter-relationship, we both became rather obsessed with the thought – or fear -- that our correspondence reflected a love-letter-writing persona, that our longing was for an imagined person, a figment of fantasy and thwarted desire. Were we each in love with a real person, or in love with being in love?

I think of you very, very often, my dear. I try to feel you - and I know it's dangerous when I try to plant you in my everyday life - in what I do and where I go, in the records I listen to, in the good pleasure I feel coming home, walking barefoot on the lawn at the perfectly peaceful hours of night. Sometimes I'm seized by the fear that it's not you I'm with. But I see no way out for us but to take the great risk of one day meeting a different person. No way out, I just hope it's really you and me we're writing about, dreaming of; it's you I miss so much; you I try to love with all of myself.

SEPTEMBER 13, 1971: DAVID

While still in Los Angeles, I got swept up in a political controversy, which involved the State of Israel giving Governor Ronald Reagan a medal of valor for signing a law to allow California banks to buy Israel bonds. I protested mockingly:

Normally, such things go to people in armies – like yourself. All well and good, but why do the Jews have to kiss his ass as if he was a great friend of ours? I'm afraid that this is an indication of how Israel (and the American Jewish community) are becoming more reactionary.

To add insult to injury, Abba Eban, then Israel's foreign minister and a hero in our eyes for his speech to the UN defending Israel on the eve of the 1967 war, was coming to personally give Reagan the award. I joined up with comrades from the Jewish Radical Community to write a fiery leaflet denouncing the award.

The thing that really pisses us off so much is the utter contempt with which Israel treats the Jews of the Galut – if they wonder why so many young Jews are turned off from Zionism and Judaism, they can find the answer right here. When are Jews going to learn that their best friends are other Jews and not the Caesars of the world? Plus ça change, plus c'est la meme chose.

Once I got this histrionic rant off my chest, I could turn to what was most on mind: Racheli's imminent induction into the Israeli army, which would have taken place by the time she received this letter:

Well, by now you must be a newly inducted member in the world's oldest profession (or is that prostitution?). No great honor but I expect that, by now, you are beyond thinking such lofty thoughts. You are probably more concerned with cleaning imaginary dirt off your imaginary boots (this army business is enough to boggle the imagination) which have to march imaginary marches in imaginary parades.

No longer do "Right" and "Left" refer to political parties; now, they distinguish between your two feet. How peculiar: in the army, your feet are the most important part of your body, while in regular life, it's your head (that's what Marx would call "inversion").

More seriously, though:

I'm scared of what the army may do to you. They want to rob you of your sensitivity, of your individuality. You have to keep a hold of that, as if it's a thread of a large piece of cloth – as long as you hold the thread, they can't take away the cloth. I hope my letters can help you keep in touch with the real world. Please try to find time between playing around with your rifle to write to me. The pen is still mightier than the sword.

I signed off in block letters: "MAKE BABIES, NOT BOMBS!"

As it happened, I was about to have my own confrontation with the army, Uncle Sam's, in my case. Since I had graduated – and there was no deferment for graduate school any longer – plus I had a drawn a low number in the draft lottery, that put me in serious jeopardy of going to Vietnam. I expected sometime in the next couple of months to have the army physical examination in Los Angeles, where my draft board was located in a federal building overlooking ... the veteran's cemetery. When I had gone to register for the draft at age eighteen, the clerk said sardonically: "This is the first stop and that – pointing out the window to the cemetery—is the last!" If I passed the physical, my choices were: the army, jail (which I considered more or less equivalent to the army), or leave the country. So, I wrote, it now became possible that I would get to Israel sooner rather than later, thus turning lemons into lemonade.

That both Racheli and I were thinking about military service at the same time highlights an important difference: the American army had become totally discredited in my eyes – and in the eyes of most of my contemporaries – but the Israeli army still had the patina of a true defense force. Yet the anti-militarism in which I had been steeped in Berkeley was something that Racheli seemed to arrive at on her own, probably partly from her parents' own humanistic sensibility as well as her year in America. She, of course, was not going to evade army service, but, as time would tell, she would not follow the well-trodden path of kibbutz youth as commanders and volunteers for elite units.

SEPTEMBER 19, 1971: RACHELI

On the day of my induction into the Israeli military, I sent David the army-issued postcard with this printed message:

The IDF congratulates you on the day of your dear one's induction to fulfill her national duty and privilege.

Together with you we hope she will be a good soldier.

In the next few days, you will be sent her military address and will be able to write to her and reply to her letters.

With greetings,

The Commander of the Induction Base

I must have gotten my hands on two postcards, since I am sure I sent one to my parents as well. I remember thinking how funny, yet touching, it was that the army required you to send a postcard home to reassure your parents that you were in safe hands.

My hand-written note was, of course, much more personal and emotional:

My David,

It's strange for me to write you in Hebrew and to write after this

day – I simply don't know what to write – only hurrying to send
you my address in the army.
You must write to me a lot, and quickly – the connection of writing
to you, waiting for a letter, sinking for one moment into our bond
– that's the rope that will occasionally pull me out, so I don't get
washed away in this deluge.
Rachel Korati (that's me)
ID # 2555279 A/1
Army Post 3051
IDF

It had been an exhausting day as the IDF transformed us from a gaggle of excited and nervous girls into female soldiers. I tried to put on airs and pretend I was not anxious by demonstratively reading a book as we passed a full day standing in multiple lines for a cursory physical exam, inoculation shots, and receiving our uniforms. The book was *I Never Promised You a Rose Garden*, a fictional tale of a young woman with what was then called split personality disorder. Nothing could have expressed better my view of what the army was about to do to me.

In remembering my days in the army, I cannot quite conjure up the feeling of dread at the start and misery as time went on, which I so often reported in my letters to David. Rather, my overall recollection is that, with the exception of having frozen toes at night and struggling at our night-time runs decked out in our heavy gear with the antiquated Czech rifles on our shoulders, the army service was generally easy for me, my duties not terribly taxing and my newly-made friends charming and supportive. Perhaps it was a bit of a pose: a manifestation of my growing Yossarian-inspired anarchism from *Catch 22*, which per David's urging earlier on, I had read and adopted as my "new bible."

As a matter of fact, serving in the army was, for my cohort of kibbutzniks, not just a mandated duty, but a calling. I joined the army at a time in Israel's history when it was still expected that every able-bodied kibbutz boy would volunteer for an elite unit and, if possible, become an officer. My oldest brother, Gil, was a company commander in the Nachal and fought in the West Bank during the Six Day War. My middle brother, Eran, who suffered from disabling asthma, served in a hush-hush division of the Air Force. I don't know for sure what he did, because when you asked him about it, he'd always say he "played bridge." But he was deployed for a long period during and following the Yom Kippur War, so I'm sure he did more than perfect his card-playing skills.

For girls, the options were more limited and most of the jobs in the army were clerical. That is why I volunteered for the Nachal, which called for a more meaningful service – a natural extension of my year as a youth movement counselor. The kind of kids I led at Ken Borochov – both boys and girls - would join the army as a group in a garin and spend most of their service together. By serving as a commander, I would be on a kibbutz movement mission to further inculcate communitarian values and inspire those under my command to be good soldiers and even better kibbutzniks. Underneath my newly acquired cynicism about armies and war, I was still an idealistic kibbutznik.

I wrote my first letter from the army the very first night at Machane Shmonim (Base #80), which is situated amidst orange groves in the long, wide valley that rolls from the foothills of the southern Carmel mountains towards the coastal plain. The nearest towns were sleepy Pardes Hannah and the not-much-livelier Hadera. It was the evening of Rosh Hashanah. Even though I was exhausted from the induction procedures, I was in a contemplative mood. I included a poem by Yehuda Amichai, whom David would meet only a few weeks later when Amichai taught for a semester in Berkeley. We shared a passion for his poetry.

I hear within me at all times a poem by Yehuda Amichai, which is my favorite poem. It's a poem called "In the Place Where We Are Right." I got attached to this poem when I wrote my Final Thesis

at school about the connection between knowing Arabs and the
attitude towards the Arab-Israeli conflict, as expressed in Hebrew
literature.

The Place Where We Are Right (I wrote it out in Hebrew; this
is my translation)

From the place where we are right
Flowers will never grow
In the spring.

The place where we are right
Is hard and trampled
Like a courtyard.

But doubts and loves make
The world porous,
Like a mole, like plowing.
And a whisper will be heard in the place
Where once stood the house
That had been destroyed.

I suppose that being inducted into the army was a poignant
moment for me, one when you needed to remind yourself that self-
righteousness hardens everything and only doubt and love soften
the world and allow flowers to grow.

SEPTEMBER 19, 1971: DAVID

While the eve of Rosh Hashanah found Racheli on her army base,
I was in Berkeley in a contemplative mood about this juncture in my
life. I tried to convey it in a poem by Yevgeny Yevtushenko:

When your face
Appeared over my crumpled life
At first I understood
Only the poverty of what I have.
Then its particular light
On woods, on rivers and on the sea
Became my beginning in the coloured world
In which I had not yet had my beginning.
I am so frightened, I am so frightened
Of the unexpected sunrise finishing,
Of revelations
And tears and the excitement finishing.
I don't fight it, my love is this fear,
I nourish it who can nourish nothing,
Love's slipshod watchman.
Fear hems me in.
I am conscious that these minutes are short
And that the colours in my eyes will vanish
When your face sets.

I had revisited our letters from the previous year. It was now just over a year since we had begun to correspond. I had saved 31 letters (was that all, or had I lost some? It certainly seemed like there had been more) and wrote: "I just was looking over the letters you had sent me last year. How childish and groping we were (and still are)!" Racheli had sent me several presents for the New Year: a book of the Song of Songs and Arik Einstein's record of children's songs. How appropriate both were for the two of us! I was deeply moved: "Sometimes you absolutely overwhelm me – and all doubts and hesitations vanish. I have an immensely warm feeling and also a sharp feeling of guilt that I don't really deserve having such a beautiful friend."

Racheli had also sent an official army photographer's picture of herself on her first day in the IDF. Despite her protestations, I found it very cute and it was very important to me, because now I had another visual reminder of the real person behind the letters.

This picture brought up a deeper issue:

I sometimes wonder about how you see yourself as a woman ... Was it silly of me to be happy when Marcie told me that you had long hair? These are, of course, external and superficial things, but a relationship of love involves many things. I think we have a very good intellectual relationship (have I ever told you that I consider you the most brilliant girl I know?) and we are in the process of developing an emotional relationship. What is lacking is anything physical. How I want to be able to touch you, feel what your skin is like – kiss you and feel you kiss me back. I have only written these things because it is the season of honesty. Wherever you've pitched your tent, please think of me and write me back.

I might as well have asked myself: "How do you see yourself as a man?"

SEPTEMBER 22, 1971: RACHELI

Right after our induction, we were sent home for a holiday for several days following Rosh Hashanah. Once back on the base, I wrote to David, trying to convey the new rhythms of my life:

The whole holiday I was busy with mending my uniform, collecting all kinds of small things that I need and other such "homework." I don't know what to tell you – you seem so far away from all this. Once again – must run to a roll call.

10:30: I'm back, but in 5 minutes it's "Lights Off." This will be a
letter-in-installments. I'll send it tomorrow in any case, so it gets
to you soon, and I'll continue in the next letter.

I quickly realized that the daily routine included a tremendous
amount of manufactured uncertainty, anxious anticipation, and
wasted time. The ultimate goal, I believed was clear, and I was onto
their scheme:

It makes you totally helpless, but I grasped the trick already a
while ago – the psychological factor is obvious – in this state of
affairs there develops a total dependency on the unit commander
while, at the same time, from the zero they have turned you into,
they build you up – as they want to, based on "platoon pride" –
now making you into a soldier. But that won't work with me – I've
discovered their secret.

I might have been onto their secret strategy, but a moment later, the
army got the upper hand: "They are already turning off our lights."

SEPTEMBER 23 - 24, 1971: DAVID

For the first – and only – time, I wrote to Racheli in Hebrew on
a typewriter which I had somehow snagged. Here is how it began
in translation:

Even though I've managed to teach myself to conquer this
technological monster, each letter comes very slowly. I was very
happy to receive the army-issued postcard. It was very cute and
reminds me of a summer camp director who makes sure that every
camper writes to his parents that everything is alright.

With this laboriously written letter, I enclosed several photos of
myself to reciprocate for those Racheli had just sent me. And in
exchange for the army postcard that I had received from Racheli , I
sent a "campy" postcard of the poster from John Wayne's 1949 movie
The Sands of Iwo Jima:

Yes, siree, you too can be a soldier like John Wayne. Sign on the
dotted line, kill ten thousand Japs with your bare hands and raise

the red-white-blue-and-yellow [a reference to a line from a song in Hair]. Seems funny that, normally, it is the boy who goes off to war and his girlfriend sits home and pines away. Now things are reversed.

In a later letter, but on the same theme, I wrote, tongue-in-cheek: "I'm no feminist. I believe that a woman's place is in the kitchen and in the army."

SEPTEMBER 25, 1971: RACHELI

"10:30: 'Lights Off' now (I am writing by flash light)," I began, expecting to write only a few lines, but somehow managed a real letter, starting in Hebrew with my favorite song of the beloved singer, Arik Einstein, which I really did take to heart at the time:

> You and I will change the world
> You and I – then everyone will come along
> It's been said already, before me
> Doesn't matter
> You and I will change the world.
>
> You and I will start all over
> We'll have it bad, no matter – it's not terrible
> It's been said already, before me
> Doesn't matter
> You and I will change the world."

Then I append this comment: "Sorry, but for the next 20 months I'm in the army – so you are it! – as far as changing the world."

Meanwhile, I was focusing on the next few days ahead of me. I was going to spend Yom Kippur on the base, which I actually considered a great opportunity. At Kfar Ruppin, Yom Kippur was just an ordinary work day. A tiny number of members did fast, so they were excused from work, but everyone else carried on as usual and there was no marking of the day in any way. Stationed at the base, I would have to fast, unless I chose to sneak some sweets I had brought from home and stashed away. But this was perhaps my opportunity for a meaningful experience. However, as the day approached, I became skeptical:

Three more days until Yom Kippur – I am eagerly anticipating seeing what will happen with me. You know, it seems to me that I focus too much on the abstract ideas – that I'll fast -- instead of the actual action itself. I am afraid of feeling a kind of emptiness.

The day after Yom Kippur, I reported:

I fasted and attended almost all the whole service at the synagogue. I don't yet know what to tell you about it – I haven't had time to think. But I think I'll fast next year, too. Throughout the whole service I was not able to get beyond just learning about it but, nevertheless, when they blew the shofar and all the young men danced and sang "Next Year in Jerusalem" there was something inside me, something moving, something new and very important and, again, I was thinking of you.

For David, too, actually perhaps more than for me, the High Holidays presented the framework for soul searching and deep feelings. "Your Rosh Hashanah letter was more than I would wish myself for the new year. I'm so thankful you're brave enough to be more honest than I. Your words, your feelings filled me up and reached all ends inside me." David's fiercely direct question about how I saw myself as a woman clearly (if in hindsight) threw me for a bit of a loop. He was asking the real, core question.

I worry about how I see myself as a woman, about how I see you as a man, about this side of our relationship, because it's the hardest to develop in writing, because I wanted it to be simple.

I wanted it to come by itself without saying it. But I know now, and I should have been honest enough to realize and admit it to myself earlier, that we are somehow ahead of ourselves, and we will have to grapple with it long before it's real. . .

I did not use at the escape hatch David had offered -- that somehow my kibbutz upbringing had made me sexually unprepared, too timid, or, more bluntly, too prudish, to think of myself, present myself, and openly talk about myself as a sexual woman: "David, it's not kibbutz education, it's going deeper into ourselves, it's making a big step in the journey further into each other, that is our difficulty." I wasn't ready to talk openly about desire and sexuality, but I hinted at it by saying: "David, we have to realize what this means because it's getting more serious as we mature." "Serious" was, obviously, my code word for love, "mature" for time to talk openly about sex. It would still take a good stretch of time before I was ready to put it into explicit words, and much longer to put words into action. I turned to the Bible to rescue me: ". . . read Psalms: 'Like a deer longs for rivulets of water; so my soul longs for you.'"

To lighten the mood, I included a self-portrait in uniform (on stationery from the education materials production workshop my father ran at Kfar Ruppin). Throughout my army service, and in later years, drawing funny cartoons – of myself or others - was always a refuge. The portrait shows one of the small ways I rebelled against the army and its often-arbitrary rules. The regulation for female soldiers held that long hair had to be gathered in a ponytail, a pinned braid or a bun. It could be kept short and loose, as long as not one hair touched the back of your collar. I grew an Afro, in concert with David growing one in Berkeley. My hair burst up above the crown of my head and jutted to the sides, but in the back, it was trimmed to exactly one centimeter above the collar. My commanding officer was scandalized and distraught, but there was nothing she could do: my hairdo met army protocol.

YOM KIPPUR, SEPTEMBER 29, 1971: DAVID

Yom Kippur, at the end of September, made me feel strangely melancholy. I expressed my mood by quoting Simon and Garfunkel, underlining September, as if to speak of our maturing love:

> April, come she will, when streams are ripe and swelled with rain.
> May, she will stay, resting in my arms again.
> June, she'll change her tune, in restless walks she'll prowl the night.
> July, she will fly, and give no warning to her flight.
> August, die she must. The autumn winds blow chilly and cold.
> September, I'll remember a love once new has now grown old.

I'm not sure why I chose such a somber song to send to Racheli. Perhaps I sensed that true love necessarily arouses the fear of loss.

I reported that in preparation for Yom Kippur, I had been studying Talmud for the first time: "I enjoyed the mental exercise, but it was hard for me to think in the Talmudic way of thought. We were studying the laws of finding things – big deal." A year later, when I was already in Israel, I took the preparatory course in Talmud at the Hebrew University, studying the laws of marriage. This time, I got bitten by the bug of talmudic study and it also proved more useful than the laws of finding things. Once we decided to marry in Israel, I had to appear in front of a rabbinic court to prove that I was Jewish and single. When I explained to the ultra-Orthodox judges that I was studying tractate Kiddushin (the laws of marriage) at the Hebrew University, the only one who spoke Hebrew (the others only spoke Yiddish) exclaimed in stunned surprise and perhaps also horror: "They teach Talmud at the Hebrew University?"

Like Racheli, I was planning to fast on Yom Kippur, although I confessed that I didn't really know why. In contrast to my later aversion to anything "synagogal," I wrote that I liked not only the feasts before and after but also the prayers at the Berkeley Hillel House. During the service, I taught the Book of Jonah, focusing on Rashi (the eleventh-century French biblical exegete), whose script I had just learned to read. The biblical text writes the word for the fish that swallowed Jonah once in the male form and once in the female. According to Rashi (based on earlier rabbinic midrash), Jonah had felt quite comfortable in the spacious belly of the male fish, so God commanded the fish to vomit him out and into the much tighter belly of a female fish. Feeling squeezed in there, Jonah began to pray. My commentary in the letter to Racheli: "Sometimes Jonah seems like a real idiot. One guy in the congregation said that Rashi's explanation was pure bullshit because science teaches us that some fish are male and female at the same time. I prefer Rashi's bullshit to that kind of science."

But as self-reflective as I aspired to be during the "Ten Days of Awe," I also kept my hand in political action. Two days before Yom Kippur, the Radical Jewish Union demonstrated at the Israeli consulate in San Francisco, awarding the State of Israel the "Golden Calf Award" for bestowing an award on Ronald Reagan (the same issue as the one I had gotten involved with in Los Angeles). This was an example of the anarchic spirit of the RJU, in this case invented by Bradley Burston, who, a life-long friend, later had a distinguished career writing for the Israeli newspaper Haaretz. Our antics got us into the newspaper. "In general, we are having our usual hilarious time and expect to get precious little studying done this year."

Despite this blithe declaration, it was, in fact, my intention to do a lot of studying that year, my first in graduate school. But I was running into some real resistance in the Berkeley History Department:

> *Various assimilated Jewish professors have been giving me the run-around about taking Jewish history. They feel it's a "narrow, specialized field." The idiots don't seem to understand that I can't waste time taking their courses when there's a tremendous amount to learn in Jewish history and literature.*

And, then, I signed off:

> *Nu, my love, I haven't heard from you for a while. Have they made you a general yet? Maybe you're too busy commanding armies and the like. Or maybe you're in army jail for forgetting to tie your shoe laces properly.*

OCTOBER 2, 1971: RACHELI

The sweet taste of freedom! "I got a 4 hour leave to go to Hadera [about a 15-minute drive from the army base] to fix my broken glasses and I have all the time free because they don't have prescription dark glasses like I need! Such freedom -- it's great." I used the unexpected break to quickly write a letter and post it in Hadera (I guess I always had an aerogram in my pocket in case the opportunity to use civilian mail arose). "I'm using the chance to send this letter through regular mail so I can now tell you all the military secrets – like – I hate it! I put Kfar Ruppin outside because I'm not supposed to use civilian mail."

When I got back to the base, I wrote a second aerogram, not as giddy, but actually rather serious and emotionally wrenching.

I feel that I owe you so much after the letter you wrote me on Rosh Hashanah, but I don't know if I can handle this. You know, sometimes I worry that the way we build up our relationship through letters, with such a space of time to think out things, so many things unsaid, left to be read between the lines, really creates, for me, such protection that I do not communicate things that scare me, the things I worry about. . .

I pleaded with David to be patient with me, despite my inability to answer him properly: "Write me a lot please, stay close to me, David, if I deserve it; because I need it."

A week later I was greatly cheered by anticipation of "friends and family visiting day" at the base:

Some people from Kfar Ruppin will come too, maybe even my mother will come! Actually, I must note that she hasn't yet spoken to the Army's Chief of Staff about the fact that her daughter is in the army. She hasn't even written to the commander of the base to keep an eye on me and, all together, she's not embarrassing me.

Another upbeat event was a trip to Afula to fix my glasses, after the failure in Hadera. This time my mission was a success, but the best part came last: "It is such a pleasure to eat ice-cream after two weeks on the base!" Somehow, telling David about the ice cream released a stream of positive feelings about my life in the army:

Tonight, we have a movie – this army is cultured! It costs 20 agorot to enter and if the movie is no good, at least the spending is worth it for hanging out with the hevre. All and all, meeting hevre whom I know here is terribly important and makes me happy each time. I have quite a lot of acquaintances here.

Among them was Ruti, from my kibbutz, who was kind enough to bring me little packages from my parents on weekends when she had leave to go home and I stayed at the base. The most precious one she delivered on my last weekend of basic training in early November: my mother's upside-down cheesecake layered with freshly picked blackberries from the wadis around Kfar Ruppin. Every bite was a taste of heaven, even though I had only a few since I felt obliged to share the cake with my tent-mates.

I even seemed to have developed a bit more distance and a sense of humor about the army routines and rigor I had complained so much about:

It turns out that the brain-washing they do here is very effective. Yesterday and today, we had good roll calls and the girls were truly happy when they were told so. You see, they've succeeded in planting in our heads the idea that it's really terribly important that the water canteen stopper is turned towards the back of the tent while the kitbag's bottom faces the tent opening, that the cup handle faces outward and that the joint connecting the handle to the mess kit faces into the tent's interior. Nu, at least one reason I can find to rejoice is that, indeed, the girls are trying harder for successful roll calls and thus, we have fewer repeat ones.

OCTOBER 2, 1971: DAVID

Since we were now writing to each other every few days, it became increasingly difficult to have a real dialogue: "I sometimes have the sense that our letters are shooting past each other without really touching." Furthermore, now that our letters went to and from the Israeli army, we found ourselves in a metaphorical *ménage à trois*:

It's funny having a third person in our relationship – ye old censor! I wonder if this "holy ghost" in our trinity really gives a damn what you are writing. Poor fellow probably feels left out because you never write anything directly to him, but, instead, only to me. He's probably jealous (I would be). Maybe you should take pity on him and write him a few kind words (maybe tell him about Yossarian censoring letters in Catch-22).

Back at the home front, the Radical Jewish Union was now in full swing. I regularly ate Shabbat dinner with six members of our group who lived together in an apartment a few blocks from my room. I reported on the first Shabbat conclave of the year: after dinner, thirty-five people crammed into the living room. The get-together had not even been advertised, so we began to worry about what would happen if it had. We had an intense discussion about what we would be doing in the coming year and I commented that we'd be lucky if we accomplished half of them. Then we sang for two hours or more. The next day, we met to study Talmud, but the day was just too beautiful, so we threw in the towel and went for a long hike in the Berkeley Hills.

The RJU was, in fact, extraordinarily active. We were all full-time students, yet we found time to publish the Jewish Radical, meet weekly and mount a variety of political actions. In our October edition, we listed some of our activities offered:

- Chug Soviet Jewry (discussion and action on Soviet Jews)
- Aliyah (discussion of various possibilities of living in Israel)
- *Ivrit* (conversations in Hebrew and "also free tutoring")
- Shira (singing "old and new songs"– mostly Hebrew songs)
- Friday Night *Sichot* (Discussions of various topics)
- Saturday evening: Havdalah followed by Café Finjan (Israeli song and dance party)
- Philosophy (reading and discussion of various Jewish and Zionist philosophers)

OCTOBER 12, 1971: RACHELI

Our correspondence had become the core of my life:

David, it's so good when I get a letter from you. Sometimes I tell myself that I need to search for what this is really about – what is this happiness that our connection brings me? But sometimes it's all so simple, totally understandable from how good it is for me.

Though I probably got more letters than anyone else in my company (and from America, at that!), I wasn't unique: all the soldiers treasured letters: from home, from a sibling serving somewhere else or already at the university, or – best of all - from a boyfriend. "The mail distribution is like a religious ceremony: all the girls standing in a circle around one girl who holds a bundle of letters with holy trepidation – and what joy!"

The letters were so vital that the night before we headed out for a week of field training on the sand dunes by the Mediterranean, which was the highlight of basic training, I was delighted to report, "it turns out this army has, despite it all, some good features and one of them is that we will be able to send mail from the field training. The other good thing is that we will <u>receive</u> mail." I then apologized, because I was writing at 12:30 am, while on guard duty: "I am sorry about my handwriting – I am writing with the paper on my knees – try to decipher it."

OCTOBER 10 (?), 1971: DAVID

My dearest Racheli,

The letter you sent me from home sent shivers up and down my back (even that picture of you with the silly hat affected me – has my Racheli grown older?). You are right. We have both matured over the last year and our feelings for each other have also matured. I think I already felt close to you when I was at Kfar Ruppin. It expressed itself in little ways: I always hoped that you would come to lunch when I finished work and, when you did, I was always so happy to see you cruising up on your bike.

When we were in Jerusalem at the end of summer (and I had cholera, remember? [actually, a mild case induced by a cholera vaccine]), I wanted very much to tell you how I was beginning to feel about you, perhaps to take you in my arms and kiss you and maybe even make love to you. Why didn't I? Maybe I sensed a hesitancy in you, that you were too young. That's why the way we

said goodbye (or didn't say goodbye) hurt me so much (I never had
the courage to tell you that until now).

And, to express my feelings, I sent Racheli a quotation from Psalm
63 (the first verse of which she had sent earlier):

> I thirst for you, my whole being longs for you,
> In a dry and parched land where there is no water.
> Because your love is better than life, my lips will glorify you.
> On my bed I remember you
> I think of you through the watches of the night.

The Psalmist, of course, was talking about his love of God; my
intention was much more carnal.

OCTOBER 16, 1971: RACHELI

I sat on the sand dunes facing the sea during our field training
and wrote to David. Perhaps staring westwards towards him inspired
me, or maybe it was the soft afternoon breezes. There was something
special about that moment, as what came out was a very emotional
letter about our relationship:

> *Your last two letters said so much. I was overwhelmed with the*
> *emotion they aroused. I somehow feel that we've come to a kind*
> *of climax. I just can't see how I'll be able to not see you, not have*
> *you right here with me in reality, instead of my imagination, for*
> *so much longer.*

For the first time, I, too, reflected back on our time together during
the summer of 1970. Perhaps I was finally able to do this because I
now felt so close to David, so reassured about our love that I finally
felt confident in its future.

> *I don't know if I can recall last summer – how I felt -- with everything*
> *in me unsaid, watching out for every movement, every possible*
> *nuance when you talk; I don't know what is more frustrating – the*
> *way we have it now with all the midrash and commentary but*

without the verse itself, or the way it was then – with no explanation.
Yes, there was a lot of hesitation on my side. It was all unadmitted
to myself for quite a while – maybe because I somehow didn't stop
connecting you strongly with Navah. And I was too young, and I
didn't know.

When I came to see you on the UJA trip, I was confused and
worried. I found out, without having had time to think about
it, that the gap between how I felt about you and what I
communicated in my letters was very great. I have never been so
nervous, so held up by emotions as that hour when I was in the
bus going to Berkeley. And I was worried because I didn't know
where you were at, because I didn't know what to expect from you.

Even as I write this today, I can conjure up that bus ride. It seemed
to take hours to get from San Francisco to Berkeley. I channeled my
anxiety about meeting David into my understandable worry about
not knowing where to get off the bus. Was "Berkeley" just one stop?
Would the driver announce it? Would I find my way from the bus stop
to his apartment? And once there . . . I wouldn't let my imagination go
any further than the initial embrace. Writing now, almost fifty years
later, it amazes me that I can't remember if we did embrace, and if
so, was it as strongly, as passionately, as I had dreamed?

OCTOBER 16, 1971: DAVID

After the crushing disappointment of our aborted meeting the
previous month, I suddenly got unexpected and thrilling news:

I almost hesitate to tell you the fantastic news for fear that
something may yet go wrong and we will be disappointed a second
time. I got a letter from Beit Berl [the Labor Party Research and
Education Institute] in Tel Aviv saying that I'm invited to come to
Israel in December and they will pay $250 of the transportation.
So, in short: "I'M COMING!!!!!!!!!!!!!!!!!!!!!!"

The conference for young activists about socialist Zionism was
scheduled from December 19 to December 31, which seemed like

a ridiculously long time. But I planned to arrive a week before the conference and stay on for a week and a half after it was over, plus most likely skip out on some sessions. Racheli would be in the non-commissioned officers training course at that point. Would she be able to get leave? If not, I would simply go AWOL myself. What if she couldn't get out of the army? I had an idea: "I'll write to Moshe Dayan and talk him into it (it's a long shot, of course, but maybe in a Jewish army, it will work)." I'm not sure if I was not actually just a tad serious.

OCTOBER 20, 1971: DAVID

While awaiting Racheli's reaction to my upcoming trip and a phone call that I proposed, I sent her a poem of my own:

> I like to ride my bike downhill
> On a cold autumn evening
> The wind whipping face and hands
> The smell of burning fall sticks flies
> From chimneys to sweeten my red nose.
>
> I like to curl up in my chair
> In the warmth of my room
> Protected from the wrath of the seasons
> Smoking my smoky pipe
> Writing these lines to you, my faraway love.

I reported on my studies: "I've been slaving away in the academic salt mines, sliding down the pipe dream of a master's in the spring." More importantly, there was the Jewish Radical. We were hard at work on it, although, as I reminded her: "a good part of the work involves a lot of fooling around." At Racheli's earlier suggestion, the group had decided to devote a whole issue to the subject of "Israel and the Galut." I was writing and rewriting an essay on the subject, whose tone, I confessed was "very pessimistic." Would she like it? I sent a copy to Kfar

David on his three-speed bicycle

Ruppin "as the army censor might be scandalized if I sent it to him."

My essay, "Between Two Messiahs," was placed on the same page as Racheli's, titled "Korati Letter from Israel." Mine ended, perhaps prophetically, with:

> In blindly walking the tightrope between Berkeley and Jerusalem, between a revolution that is over and one that may never come, I know that I have not found a secure, happy berth. Like the generation of the early Zionist writer, Y.H. Brenner, we are faced with Zionism as an essentially tragic choice, leading not to utopia but to inescapable struggle.

I also enclosed some pictures I had developed in the darkroom at the university: "One of the subjects is known to you – in fact, you have known her your whole life [I'm not sure when I had taken this picture]. The other one is of the hevre in an early Zionist pose. We're going to make a poster of it." We had all dressed up as early *halutzim* (pioneers) in *kaffiyas*, a toy rifle, etc. and posed on the Berkeley campus. It was a pretty successful imitation of the original photographs of that type and it's still up on the wall of my study today (next page).

The Radical Jewish Union, October 1971
Seated front (left to right): David, Timbergs' dog, Ken Bob.
Kneeling (left to right): Jane Rubin, Miri Gold, Bradley Burston.
Standing (left to right): Elaine Schlackman, David De Nola, Marcie Lincoff,
David Lichtenstein, Arnie Druck, Jack Morgenstern, Buddy Timberg,
Judy Timberg, Shaul Osadchey

OCTOBER 23, 1971: RACHELI

Not yet aware that David was coming in December, I wrote: "I felt like you have come much closer to me, not only emotionally but somehow in reality too. I found myself held much more firmly in our ties, feeling you with me or missing you much more intensely." To express this sentiment, I sent David a love poem by Leah Goldberg:

Let us remember the beginning of our love
When it was still a shy doe
A lovely antelope, her eyes downcast.

And behold, it has grown greatly
Its face is open
And its voice deep.
Its seasons are lovely.

By an amazing coincidence, I came back to this poem just before this writing. A friend commissioned me to make a calligraphed artwork for her brother and sister-in-law's 40th wedding anniversary. We wanted a Hebrew poem that was not a dewy-eyed glorifying of the blush of first romance but one celebrating a mature, life-long love. We settled on this very Leah Goldberg poem and I liked what I produced so much that I made another version for us! And, then, only a month after I completed this project, I encountered the poem in this letter. The poem was a promise, but there was still a long road ahead.

OCTOBER 24, 1971: RACHELI

The next day *everything* changed! "Today I got your letter, in Hebrew, and when I said the words 'He's coming to Israel,' my David – I simply cried, and also laughed – and I felt so well, so, so well." I described my state of mind by quoting Psalms (in hindsight, I am rather amazed at how often we resorted to quoting Biblical passages to express our most intense and intimate emotions): "When God shall return us to Zion, <u>we shall be like dreamers.</u>"

But I could not avoid anxiety:

I am scared, scared that we won't have enough time together, scared that we won't have the patience in our short time together to hold the ends of our threads with the delicacy required, with great caution, with enough love. But, David, I am so happy. Right now, it's just good. I am waiting for you so much, as always, but now it's real, so concrete, you can count the days.

OCTOBER 26, 1971: RACHELI

But then:

I'm so depressed today. I have had bad news. I talked to my commanding officer today about the chances of me getting special leave when you come. She said I'll probably get a few hours to meet you when you arrive, besides regular Hanukkah leave, if it falls in between those dates.

What a blow! I tried to soften it by saying there was something of a chance that my new commanding officer – by the time of David's visit I would be in the midst of my NCO training – would "be kind, not rigid (unlike my present one), and somehow I would get friendly - as much as one can – with the officer." I ended with a "chin up" exhortation – as much to myself as to David: "David, please try not to be too sad – we'll have to find our way through this with happiness, protect ourselves from frustration."

The worries about not getting enough leave time from the army to make the visit really meaningful and satisfying were only half of my anxiety. Just as much nervous energy and distraught writing – actually probably more – went into fear of disappointing David and, in retrospect, myself:

David, you know, it's absurd, but in a way, I find that somehow inside me I don't want you to come. I'm so scared that I will disappoint you. I'm so scared that the fantasy I've created and have been living in for so long will crash down and I don't want it to, I don't want to lose my dream!

I have no idea of how we'll be able to pour everything into a small number of hours or days. And maybe, more than anything else, I don't want you to come because you'll have to leave.

I'm thinking about what I just wrote and it seems to me I'm trying to bring up all my fears. Maybe because I lead myself to a belief that, this way, I may prevent the fear, depression and worries when you so come. It's like primitive tribes - before they go hunting, they shout out loud the names of the animals to be hunted.

OCTOBER 26, 1971: DAVID

Our RJU group had attended several lectures by visiting Israelis and Palestinians, in particular by Amos Kenan, the writer and artist, who had been a member of the Lehi, Revisionist underground and later an activist on the Left: "While I'm interested in the Israeli 'New Left,' of course, every time I hear one of these birds speak, it's a bore. Especially Kenan, who's a cold fish if ever I've seen one." However, I found myself pretty much agreeing with Kenan's position:

There were a bunch of Israeli students in the audience who got very upset at him because he is too radical for them and there were several big arguments where both sides acted like idiots: instead of arguing rationally, they just tried to make the other side look stupid. I raised my hand and said that after listening to all the stupidity, I could understand why the level of public debate in Israel was so low. That didn't gain me great popularity among the Israelis, but the RJU people there said: "right on!"

Seems like I had, maybe still have, a knack for alienating both the far Left and Right, but, at the same time, expressing the views of my close friends.

On the subject of Israel, I also reported on reading a biography of Theodore Herzl, whom I described as "a first-class creep who wanted to go to the Pope and arrange for a mass conversion of the Jews." The time had come, I thought, to reevaluate Herzl's place in Zionist history by a radical Jewish historian not willing to swallow Zionist propaganda. I proposed it to my new friend, Fred Rosenbaum, the only other graduate student pursuing Jewish history in the Berkeley History Department and, to this day, one of my closest friends. If Fred wouldn't do it, maybe I should?

Having cleared away all this political and historical underbrush, I turned to what was most important: Racheli's beautiful letter written by the Mediterranean shore, while on field exercises. This was a crucial letter in which, responding to mine, she described her own feelings about the two of us from my month at Kfar

Ruppin in August 1970 and her visit to Berkeley in February 1971.
I wrote:

> *When I said that you were young, I meant that it was probably the*
> *first time you had a relationship with a boy (am I wrong?). I never*
> *really had a meaningful, close relationship, except with one girl*
> *three years ago where we really were in love (I believe), but she was in*
> *love with this other guy. They're now married; so it goes [a reference*
> *to Kurt Vonnegut's Slaughterhouse Five]. I feel badly about Navah*
> *because I don't think I ever had any romantic interest in her and*
> *I'm afraid that she thought I did. I think maybe she hasn't written*
> *me in the past year because she is jealous that we have become so*
> *close. I wish I could see her and talk to her about that.*

As it happened, Navah went on to marry Udi de-Shalit whom she
had known since age three. His father, Amos de-Shalit, was in charge
of the Weizmann Institute physics education project initiated by her
father, Uri Haber-Schaim, in which Racheli's father participated. So,
the circles intersected. We remain close to both Navah and Udi to
this day.

OCTOBER 30, 1971: DAVID

> *"There's magic in the sleepiness of waking to a childish sounding*
> *yawn" (Eric Anderson).*
> *This morning I didn't awake to a "childish sounding yawn," but to*
> *your voice. As soon as the phone rang, I knew it was you. It was*
> *wonderful to hear your voice. It gives me a shock to realize that*
> *there's a voice behind the wonderful letters I've been getting from*
> *you.*

Indeed, talking on the phone made Racheli more real. But what I had
in addition, which she did not have, was friends who had met her
and with whom I could talk about our relationship, although they
were probably getting sick of hearing my pining and longing. And
by now, I had a definite itinerary for my trip: "Arrive Tel Aviv BOAC
flight #314 from London at 6:30 pm [no arrival date, because I must

have relayed it in my phone call – probably December 12 or 13.].
Leave January 14 or 15."

NOVEMBER 1, 1971: DAVID

To Racheli's warning that her commander might not give her any
special leave, I could only say, even though I didn't really believe it:

*I guess I'm quite fatalistic about this at this point. I will be in
Israel for four Shabbats and, according to the midrash, Shabbat is
one-sixtieth part of the world to come. So, even if we get only two
Shabbats, it's already one-thirtieth of the world to come – that's
really not so bad.*

Like her, I struggled with the difficulty of maintaining our intense
relationship through letters:

*I have felt at various points the desire to leave our relationship on
the level that it was last year (that is, lukewarm). Maybe I could
start a relationship with someone else, so that these problems
wouldn't exist. But, for some reason, I just couldn't do it. I felt that
I had with you a special relationship that was both intellectual
and emotional (a rare combination!). I feel that way now, which is
why I find myself writing to you every day, thinking about you all
the time. Please be happy. I know things will work out somehow.*

There really was no turning back.

As a token of my love, I sent Racheli a beautiful poem by Yehuda
Amichai, whose seminar I was attending. When we studied two of
his poems, he asked us with a deadpan expression: "What does the
poet mean here?" I was very taken with him.

*He is a very nice person, very German, very European and
not Israeli. I found him quite charming but somehow a little
withdrawn. You would have to know him a long time to learn as
much about him as you could learn by reading his poetry.*

When I met Amichai several times in later years, I realized that this
description was completely off the mark: he was very funny and
outgoing.

Perhaps inspired by my contact with a real poet, I felt moved to send Racheli a rather bad poem of my own, which I had written and dedicated to her the previous June, but had not dared to send at that time:

To Rachel

Each beautiful dawn above Jerusalem
Succeeds its brother
And I have missed them all.

I sit watching a shadow of myself
As I drink this wine
And write this poem
By your candlelight.

In the infinity of doubt
I am cradled
Soft, I come upon the endless night
This life is without past or future.

Can your light break through
This blinding cloud?

NOVEMBER 1 – NOVEMBER 2, 1971: RACHELI

Two days after we had talked on the phone, I wrote: "I felt very close to you with no worry, all very simple. What would it be like to be with you? As beautiful as it is in my imagination?" My sunny mood was helped by the fact that I was only ten days away from finishing basic training. The finale actually promised to be exciting:

We start out on a three-day hike – if it hadn't been with the army, it would have been great – in the Carmel mountains. We come back Thursday, go home Friday – Sat. and then there's only

4 MORE DAYS! So, you can be very happy for me Wednesday afternoon and think of me marching in formation, with uniform suit starched, my shoes shining, looking for my parents in the audience, trying to smile in the burning sun.

I had to organize and pack up the supplies for the three-day hike for my whole company, because, since I was a kibbutznik, everyone assumed I could do things like that. It was actually a huge job between food, water, medical supplies, guns and ammunition (not that we would use the guns... but we had to carry the full gear). And, needless to say, I wasn't relieved of any of the regular annoyances of roll call and practicing marching in formation. So, I was totally frazzled and exhausted:

Last night we put our equipment in storage. On the way back I put my hand in my pocket and find two letters – one that I wrote to you and one that I wrote to my parents at home. At that moment I passed a garbage can and, with no trouble, simply tossed them into the garbage. That's how it is with me now. Next, I climbed into the garbage can to fish out the letters and it's from there that the letter reaches you.

NOVEMBER 6, 1971: RACHELI

Back from the three-day hike and letter-writing hiatus, I returned to my persistent worry, but now I was finally able to be more direct and explicit:

It can be summed up in one question I need to ask you. You asked me about it and I need your answer for that: how do you see me as a woman? More likely, David, I have to know what you expect from me as a woman. Honestly, I can hardly picture what it would be like to be in your arms, to kiss you. I'm young. I have no experience of a relationship with such sexual significance as ours, and the emotional build up with it.

You are 3 years older than I – it's a lot, I don't know where you stand in terms of experience, expectations. I'm worried because

I fear I'm unprepared for your sexual maturity. It's a very hard thing to prepare for because I'm so scared one of us will come out disappointed, hurt. Please, help me in this.

NOVEMBER 6, 1971: DAVID

I should congratulate you since you are now a GRADUATE. Did you wear a cap and gown and march down the aisle while the orchestra played the March from Aida? More likely, they made you march back and forth showing off your newly-polished rifles to the admiring applause of family and friends. Wish I could have been there to hold up a sign: "MAKE BABIES, NOT BOMBS!"

Meanwhile, I had fallen behind in my reading due to working non-stop on the Jewish Radical. Graduate school, I wrote, was all about reading books and one-upping other students, which I illustrated by the following imaginary dialogue between two graduate students:

GS#1: "I just finished reading Crapper's new book on Diarrhea in Outer Mongolia. Do you know it?

GS#2: "Of course, but you know, of course, that his thesis has been totally refuted by a new book that hasn't been published yet, but you can find articles in the Excretory Review.

GS#1 [not wanting to admit that he had never heard of this journal]: "I'll have to look at that. By the way, I hear you're writing about the history of the horseshoe in southern Germany. How's it going?

GS#2: I've been working it for four years and I think it's going to be entirely original.

GS#1 [snickering in his beard]: "I'm awfully sorry, old fellow, but B.M. Cow has just published a book on that subject and I hear it's excellent.

GS#2 turns pale white, realizing he's just wasted four years of his life and runs off to live on a kibbutz.

The last part of this dialogue was based on what might have been an apocryphal story about a Berkeley history graduate student who had worked ten years on a dissertation, only to find out that someone else had scooped him.

And on the subject of graduate school, I concluded: "send me your new address for wherever you're doing 'graduate studies.'"

NOVEMBER 12, 1971: RACHELI

"Wednesday, there was a big parade – Graduation roll call on the football field of Pardes Hannah's high school. It wasn't too bad because it was short and my family came and some other friends of mine." Not exactly a big deal, but then I spilled the beans, even as I tried to downplay it as much as possible:

> *There was just one thing – I came out as the "outstanding cadet" of my platoon (you wouldn't have believed it, would you have?). So, they called out my name and I had to yell "Yes, sir" and run to the front of the "dignitaries' stage" where all the "big generals" stood, stand there and wait for all the other "outstanding cadets." The Commander in Chief of the Nachal came, gave me this piece of paper that looks like a youth movement award for taking first place in sports in a summer camp – for being an outstanding cadet - shook my hand, asked where I am from blah-blah. I then ran back to my place. End of the torture.*
>
> *How come I got the outstanding cadet award? Well, NOT because the cup on my bed was always turned the right way, not even because I participated and knew the answers during our "lessons" – I always slept through them. How? Well, I was elected by the girls only, and we were told to choose who'd helped others, volunteered, raised the morale. Well, being a kibbutz product, how could I not be all that?*

NOVEMBER 12, 1971: DAVID

As the time of my visit came nearer, our letters became more intense. Racheli's short letter of November 6 had hit me very hard and clearly accelerated our opening up to each other. She had now responded with great honesty to my earlier question of how she saw herself as a woman. We could no longer avoid thinking about a sexual relationship. She saw me as much more experienced than her, but, to tell the truth, despite a number of dalliances, I was almost as inexperienced. I could not avoid now thinking about myself as a man and how I related to women:

> *This society tends to make us split personalities (maybe Israeli society does the same thing, I don't know). On the one hand, we learn about all the virtues of love and closeness emotionally to another person. But, then, we learn from advertising and the whole social scene in American high schools (dating, etc.) that the most important thing is physical beauty and sex. As a result, I think we all feel a split between love and sex.*

The few sexual experiences I had had were unsatisfying, I thought, because they weren't based on love. Sexuality for me was the physical expression of deep emotional connection, rather than just the physical act by itself. I was not as much of a 60's radical as I thought.

I felt that we had formed a very healthy emotional relationship and I was now noticing something very interesting: "When I get a good letter from you, I wish you could be here so that I could touch you, hold you. I am finding you more sexually attractive the more you express yourself to me emotionally and intellectually." Even the most abstract or intellectual letters had that effect on me.

> *I think that you are a very, very attractive girl [no one I knew was saying "woman" yet] and you have greater capacity to love than I do. Part of this I get from your letters and part from your parents. I don't know if you ever noticed how loving your parents are toward each other, how they hold hands, touch each other. Love is never a matter of experience. It comes from openness and willingness to express yourself physically to another person. Racheli, my dearest, I want you to show me how to love you and I will try to teach you how to love me.*

NOVEMBER 20, 1971: RACHELI

I had had a ten-day leave at the end of basic training before I had to go back to Machane Shmonim and start my Non-Commissioned Officers training. I was certainly not looking forward to returning to my army life and the much more rigorous military training and discipline I was anticipating. NCO training was reputed to be nearly as hard as officers' training, without the "glory" of having what we cynically called *barzelim* ("irons"), that is, the metal insignia bars on the shoulder epaulets that officers wore. All you got as an NCO were three white stripes on your sleeve. But my spirits were buoyed by David's impending visit.

Look at the date – it's another month. I can hardly believe it – I'll be with you, together, it will be beautiful, it has to be! So much of my worries, sometimes it seems to me that they are enlarged so much because I try to live ahead of time, but things will turn out simple and good when they happen.

Surely, my optimism about our visit was in part due to the letters we had just exchanged about how we saw each other sexually:

Your letter was the letter I hoped to get as a reply. Thinking about it, it makes me feel very secure with you, realizing I wasn't worried at all about how you would accept me – how you would reply – the problem was facing myself. I have a lot of confidence in you, in your understanding – in how close and honest you are with me, and I'm very thankful for it.

NOVEMBER 22, 1971: DAVID

I was now becoming seriously worried about my own draft status. I had just received a 1A classification, which made me officially cannon fodder. Now, the only thing standing between me and Vietnam was the army physical, which I desperately hoped would not be scheduled while I was in Israel (I didn't know anyone equivalent to Moshe Dayan in the US Army to write to). I had various schemes for how to fail the physical but no certainty that they would work.

Racheli had just received the "outstanding cadet" award for her basic training, which led me to some droll ideas:

Hey, if you're so well loved by all those tin-horned generals, maybe you can cash in on this paper and convince them to give you a long leave when I come. After all, if you're such a great soldier, you obviously don't need as much training as everyone else!

I advised her to hang onto the award in case she ever found herself in the desert without essential paper.

NOVEMBER 22, 1971: RACHELI

In NCO training, I was back to writing in a few snatched moments between roll call, brain-numbing classes, marching around the camp in formation, and purging the same old Czech rifles of the last speck of sand. Our days were packed from dawn to "lights out" at 10:00 pm, so writing a real letter was a challenge. I promised to write one on Shabbat, when, even though I was to remain at the base, we were generally free unless "we have to work in the kitchen or guard some end of this base – make sure the fence doesn't move or the trees grow." In addition, once a week, we had night guard duty, which was a running joke for female soldiers. We were issued two bullets that would presumably work in our antique rifles. For safety, they were stashed in a plastic bag. We joked that if we heard suspicious sounds or saw a figure in the dark, we would call out "Halt! Halt or I'll open the plastic bag!"

NOVEMBER 28 – DECEMBER 1, 1971: DAVID

God may not play dice with the universe, but he was certainly wreaking havoc with our plans:

The conference at Beit Berl was just canceled! I couldn't believe it when I heard the news: we seem to have such incredibly bad luck with my coming to Israel. Sometimes, I think that some mysterious power is telling us that we shouldn't be together, that all this is a series of bad omens. But then I think there is no such power, just our own personal will. If we really believe we have a future, then we can overcome all obstacles. I don't know -- sometimes I look into the future and am afraid of what I see. Everything seems so uncertain, so confusing.

Because Racheli was unable to write frequently at the start of her training, I felt very alone in facing this new crisis. Our relationship was now really being put to the test:

It is very difficult not hearing from you – my imagination begins to run wild. If our relationship has become too much of an emotional burden for you, then I will understand if you want to break it off. Racheli, I'm so afraid I'm losing you.

I now regretted even more that I didn't tell her how I had felt about her when she was in Berkeley in February. I now proposed coming in March for Passover for a full three weeks.

Sometimes, though, bad news also has a silver lining:

I want to tell you what my wonderful friends from the Radical Jewish Union did for me when they heard that the conference had been canceled. They gave me an envelope with $90 in it and insisted that I go to Israel to see you. I told them that they were crazy but they wouldn't take the money back. I was really moved and didn't know how to thank them.

The group's investment in our relationship paid off.

NOVEMBER 30, 1971: RACHELI

I recovered from the crushing news of David's canceled trip faster than I would have expected. But now that our meeting was put off for a while, I worried that our letters would revert to their earlier routine and lose their intimacy. They had certainly become more intimate as we anticipated David's visit, feeling that "we had a limited time to prepare ourselves for something new." Nevertheless, I began to think practically about how a spring visit might work:

I sent you the telegram today. You know, thinking about it -- even though it means waiting another four months or whatever – when

you come on Passover, I will be an NCO already. I'll be able to get
leave for the evening almost every day and have every weekend off.

DECEMBER 4, 1971: DAVID

My course was now set. I would come to Israel for Passover and,
to do that, I would try to finish all my work early. I had to write a long
research paper for a two-quarter seminar on ethnic intellectuals in
Imperial Russia, which involved a lot of laborious reading in Hebrew
newspapers from the 1860 and 1870s. I anticipated being able to
arrive in the middle of March and to stay for around three weeks. It
was going to be hard to wait, but at least this time, we weren't going
to let any outside forces interfere with our plans.

In addition to my academic work, I was teaching a Sunday
school class at Beth El, the local Reform synagogue, on Holocaust
literature and Soviet Jewry. I was also teaching an informal study
group, composed mostly of members of the RJU, on modern Jewish
history focused on Zionist thinkers: "So far, we have demolished
Herzl, Ahad Ha'am (the pompous asshole), Berdichevsky (official
Zionist nut) and next week we are studying Rav Kook."

DECEMBER 5, 1971: DAVID

Trying to lift my spirits as I faced the US Army Draft Office
the next day, I sent a postcard of Shirley Temple playing *The Little
Colonel* with this message: "We love you, Shirley Temple, symbol of
American innocence gone sour. Tomorrow I take my draft physical
– here's hoping I'll be sicker than ever in my life. Be well and happy,
my little 'Colonel.' Love, David"

DECEMBER 6, 1971: DAVID [IN HEBREW] ON OFFICIAL STATIONERY:

Department of the Army
Armed Forces Examining and Entrance Station
4277 Wilshire Boulevard

Los Angeles, California 90005

To my Racheli, shalom,

I am sitting right now in this most shitty place in Los Angeles. A few moments ago, I finished the psychometric test of this wonderful army of ours. But the main thing: <u>I am exempt and released from the army</u>!!!!!!!!

This news was just revealed to me about an hour ago by a doctor here who reviewed all my paper work and then announced to me that my eyes are bad enough that the army doesn't want me. Of course, I was terribly disappointed, but I didn't complain – if that is, in fact, my fate, I will gladly accept it! I'll tell you my trick – I am using a pair of glasses with a little bit stronger prescription than my regular ones.

<u>Evening</u>

I had to stop the letter because I was brought the results of the psychometric test. Evidently, I got a high enough score to qualify for at least an NCO course, if not an officers' course, too bad, but I have to decline this "honor."

Now I am in the midst of traveling by air to Berkeley – tired but rather satisfied by the results of this "Judgment Day." Well. We are landing. Wow! What a beautiful view of the Bay and the towns around it. Everything is crystal clear. You can see the bridge over the Bay like a thread of light. You know what, my dear? There are times when I really love San Francisco and this whole area. But, nevertheless, I also pine for you and your country.

DECEMBER 6, 1971: RACHELI

Life in the army had certainly changed my criteria of comfort and pleasure:

A very rare free evening as it has been pouring all day long and all plans were changed. We were supposed to start 8 days of field training (same story as in basic training) but didn't. So, I am sleeping in a bed (!) with sheets, electricity and other luxuries

instead of in mud in a one-meter-tall tent that's about to fly off
any moment. I'll do that next week I think, I hope it will be better
than what I picture in my imagination right now.

Ever since those days, sleeping in a bed with clean sheets has been a
pleasure I appreciate every night. David is probably rather tired by
now of my nightly satisfied sigh, "Ummm. . . I love my bed!" although,
sweetly, he never complains. I ended my letter with a verse from the
Song of Songs verse: "On my bed at night, I seek the one my soul loves."

DECEMBER 8, 1971: RACHELI

I was very moved by the news that David's friends from the RJU
had collected money to send him to me: "I had such a warm feeling
when I read about your hevre." And, yet, I was experiencing a kind
of struggle with my feelings and admitted:

I have withdrawn in a way – at some point haven't fulfilled a
certain commitment to openness, to giving as much as I was
receiving from you. I feel very bad about it.

The past two weeks – for several reasons (cancellation of your trip,
very tight schedule here), I haven't come to a point where I felt I
could weigh things. Nothing was ripe enough. It is very hard to
adjust to the thought of waiting another three months.

Nevertheless, I tried to respond to some of the issues David had
been struggling with in letters from a while back regarding his future
trajectory. In hindsight, I think I felt it was important to address these
before David came for his visit, so there wouldn't be an elephant in
the room and our time together would be the pure joy I was dreaming
of. Here, I thought I had it much easier: my life for the next year-
and-a-half was predetermined by the army, and my assumption was
that after that I would follow the typical kibbutznik's path: a year
or two of working at Kfar Ruppin, then applying to the university
and negotiating with the kibbutz higher education committee what
I would study. It would have to be something useful to the kibbutz,
so that the General Assembly (which met every Saturday night and

made all major decisions for the community) would approve my plans.

David's conflicted feelings about his future were of utmost importance to me. A part of me, even though not yet fully articulated, knew I wanted our futures to be bound together. As was my wont, I addressed this through an ideological lens:

> *I really want to discuss the kibbutz with you because it seems to me that, at certain points, questioning yourself and where you're heading, you sometimes point to kibbutz life as one of the last alternatives and some kind of an answer, some end of a rope to pull yourself out of a frightening feeling of empty spaces in front of you.*
>
> *I ask myself – and I have to be absolutely honest with you, I pray this doesn't hurt you - whether you're not constantly postponing a completely honest and thorough consideration of the question of kibbutz to reassure yourself you have enough possible answers to your loneliness and fears, but it's not so for me.*
>
> *When I face my doubt, I find answers when I daydream, picturing a morning hike on Shabbat with my children in the fishponds, or listening to them talk about what happened at school that day, or breakfast together on the lawn in the sun*
>
> *My parents really show me so much in the kind of life they lead. I think they have found a very satisfying answer to the dilemma you are (and I am too) so troubled by: a combination of very intensive intellectual activity together with building little things in everyday life.*
>
> *A few months ago, I came home for Shabbat. My parents and I went hiking to pick blackberries [still an obsession of mine!]. I was sincerely happy. It was so good being together, such a feeling of accomplishment, of closeness, and this is where I find answers. I feel you have those answers lying deep inside you. It has to be among the things I love about you.*

DECEMBER 11, 1971: RACHELI

In a romantic mood, I wrote to David from the exact spot on the beach where I'd been sitting two months earlier:

Shabbat. The same place on the seashore I once wrote you from – "field training" – remember?

This morning I got up at 5:45 and slipped out of my tent. It was just before sunrise. I snuck out of the camp, sat on a small hill and watched. The sun rising, like the daffodils blooming at the side of the road we saw walking here Thursday, like the singing last night in the darkness, all make me so much more aware of how I need you with me.

Is it strange that beauty arouses in me very strong emotional and sexual feelings for you?

You have no idea how I wish to take a walk with you in our hills at home when they're blooming with anemones, just walking – early in the morning, holding your hand, in silence.

We still take such walks, but never that early in the morning.

DECEMBER 12, 1971: DAVID

Dearest Racheli,

Yes, I understand exactly how you feel from your letter written on Shabbat, Dec. 4. It's like we were filling a balloon and just when it was ready to pop, someone started letting the air out very slowly, which is more painful. Love should be an absence of tension, a perfect harmony, but we are gripped by a greater tension than if we didn't have each other. Even though a lot of tension remains when we are open and honest, it is a "better" tension than if we are not saying anything.

Well, winter has finally come to Berkeley – lots of rain dripping against my window as I lie in bed, half here and half someplace else. Very appropriate: Handel's Water Music on the record player.

DECEMBER 18, 1971 - SHABBAT, 7TH CANDLE [OF HANUKKAH], MIDNIGHT: RACHELI

I had not written in five days because during the field training week I had no time and no light at night:

Would you understand what it's like if I told you I hardly had time to read your letters? I carry your letters with me all the time in case we get a few minutes off, so I can read them. I couldn't read at night because we had no light, we lost our candles - yes, it was that bad. The hard thing to take is that I spent all that time cleaning up rifles with endless amount of oil, rust and sand, turning my helmet into a bush (camouflage!), digging trenches, and other very important missions I'm sure Israel's security depends on.

A depressing state of affairs, but we did receive mail out in the field, and that included a wonderful surprise: "in the middle of all this I get an Almond Joy – do you realize what it means, my dear? I couldn't be happier." Almond Joy was my favorite American candy bar during the year we spent in Boston, so, despite the much-too-sweet goo that was the bulk of it, my attachment to it was fierce, like how one feels about an old love of one's youth. I can no longer tolerate the excessive sweetness, but thinking of it still makes me feel happy, almost swoon. And David, knowing about this particular sweet tooth, had smuggled one into a small package. But, of course, much more important and sweeter, was David's letter from the Draft Office announcing he had been found unsuitable. What a moment of relief that was!

I returned to the subject of our sexual relationship, that is, the imagined one we were fantasizing and worrying about. To express my feelings of inexperience, I drew, once again, from the Song of Songs:

I like the imagery in The Song of Songs: "A locked garden is my sister-bride." It seems like sexual relations are something like walking through a garden. The first time you look at every little flower on your side -- every touch and smile is a flower you pick. And even though you tell yourself that the farther in you go the

more beautiful and amazing the flowers are, you cannot take
another step before you've studied all that is around you. That's
how I picture it – am I wrong?

DECEMBER 22, 1971: DAVID

I returned from an exhausting but satisfying five-day winter
camp to find Racheli's beautiful letter from December 11. I found
very affecting her remarks on beauty arousing such strong feelings
of sexual and emotional desire:

The only way to really appreciate beauty is to share it with someone
you love. If I listen to a beautiful piece of music or go walking in the
hills in the spring, if I do it by myself, I still feel as if it is distant from
me. That is why beauty produces in me at the same time feelings of
happiness and loneliness. The only way to overcome that feeling is
to share it with someone you feel absolutely comfortable touching.
Then you can touch what is beautiful by touching the person you
are sharing it with. It is as if you can break down the wall that
separates you from the rest of the world only with someone else.

I especially appreciated her mention of fields of anemones because,
since the age of nine when I spent the year in Israel, that flower had
aroused in me the strongest emotions.

Our relationship was now put to a different test, however. At
the winter camp, one of the counselors, named Debbie, and I were
attracted to each other. After the camp, I told her openly that I was
deeply committed to a woman in Israel and that I would only know
for sure where I stood once she and I were able to see each other in
March. Debbie and I continued to see each other off and on during
the winter, but with clear boundaries: nothing could happen between
us until I returned from Israel in early April.

DECEMBER 24, 1971: DAVID

On "Erev Christmas," as I put it, mixing two religions, I reported
that I was like Piglet in Winnie-the-Pooh, "entirely surrounded by

water." It was raining and raining. To celebrate the birth of that "radical Jew, 1971 years ago," I was listening to Handel's Messiah and had also baked a cake, "which is good but not as good as the Messiah. Nu, what else is new? Man does not live on bread alone ... but also on cake."

DECEMBER 25, 1971: RACHELI

Writing on Christmas Day meant nothing in Israel. I didn't even note it, but did mention I was writing the letter "in bed in my tent – at the base, raining outside," just like in Berkeley. It was Shabbat, which was the time I could write a serious letter. So, I wrote further about insecurity around sexuality:

I'm asking myself what's behind this insecurity: fears about sex or maybe just a way of growing up with people on kibbutz. Even Bettelheim [Bruno Bettelheim in his important book about kibbutz education, Children of the Dream] says something about this. He says that growing up in a tight-knit society where sexual feelings towards the other sex in your peer group are almost taboo, somehow causes some repression of sexual feeling in other relations too. I don't know – maybe this is very superficial. I think I would have more of an answer when these problems are dealt with in reality.

Indeed, but that reality was still months away.

DECEMBER 29, 1971: DAVID

Working feverishly on my research seminar paper had awakened my chronic questioning about academic life. Was I doing something meaningful or would it be better to throw it all away and do something in the "real" world? I apologized to Racheli for troubling her with this ambivalence, a recurring subject between us:

Sometimes I think you're crazy to like me. I think I'm much less confused about my life than most American kids, but wouldn't you prefer to be involved with some Israeli guy who doesn't feel or, at least, doesn't express all these ambiguities and problems?

I feel very happy to have someone like you who is so stable and certain of herself. I wonder if there is some comparable reason why you like me?

Actually, I'm doing something really dumb. I'm thinking about you in that classic stereotype of the Israeli who doesn't express his emotions or his doubts. But I know you're not like that at all, my Racheli, which is why I feel so close to you even though you're far away.

DECEMBER 31, 1971: DAVID

I felt I had to write more on the question of sexual experience: "What is experience anyway? It only helps in a relationship with one person, because each new relationship is different, feels different, has its own needs, its own particular experiences." The Song of Songs metaphor of erotic love as a garden struck me as beautifully evocative:

Yes, we will go walking in the garden together, I hope. It doesn't matter whether I have been there before (after all, I don't know it much better than you), because we must both walk at the same pace, not too slow and not too fast. And you mustn't think that the flowers at the entrance are any less important than those further along the path – each time we explore them together, it is as if we have never seen them before. Are you willing to walk with me, holding my hand, teaching me to look at the flowers just as I teach you?

Chapter 5

GREAT EXPECTATIONS
January-March 1972

JANUARY 3, 1972: DAVID

A new year and, I hoped, a more successful one for our budding relationship than the last. I was quite interested in what Racheli wrote about sexual repression on kibbutz and suggested that she ask her mother about it. Of course, just talking about it with her mother would be proof that such repression was not total. However, as I would learn in later years, Anina, Racheli's mother, was anything but representative of kibbutzniks. She was an iconoclast in every respect and about as open about sex as anyone I've ever met. She was even the "designated person" giving sex education talks to prepubescent kids on the kibbutz, something Racheli was both proud of and embarrassed about growing up (only the former feeling, of course, remains with her as an adult). Unbeknownst to me at the time, the subject of sexuality among the founders of the kibbutz movement would become a chapter entitled "Zionism as an Erotic Revolution" in my 1992 book, *Eros and the Jews.*

I had just completed a bibliographical paper on the German General Staff between 1871 and 1905:

> *Perhaps your army group would like me to give a lecture on this timely military subject. I can tell them why the German army decided to invade France in 1914 and why the Israeli army shouldn't, even if it can't get back the money for those Mirages [Charles de Gaulle had imposed a boycott of military arms to Israel after the Six Day War and had not delivered Mirage jets that Israel had paid for].*

JANUARY 6, 1972: DAVID

My letter raised for the first time the idea of forming a garin from the RJU. A few years later, when we were already students in the US, we would play a key role in founding *Garin Tohu*, named in a nod to anarchism and provocation, after Genesis 1: the *Tohu Va-Vohu* (helter skelter) of the world prior to creation. Our plan was to make *aliyah* and join Kibbutz Gezer, half-way between Tel Aviv and Jerusalem. During the 1948 war, the kibbutz was overrun by Arab forces after a long and bloody battle, in which 39 Haganah and kibbutz members were killed. One of those casualties was a relative of Racheli's, so Gezer had a special meaning for her.

The kibbutz was reestablished in 1964 but struggled for its economic and social survival. In 1974, a garin of Americans preceded ours to revive Gezer. We knew many of them from the Zionist youth movement and Jewish student movement in the US. Our garin was the natural second wave. But shortly before our group picked up *en masse* and went to Israel in 1976, we dropped out. In some ways we were heart-broken and disappointed in ourselves, but we had realized that we were on a different track. Some of our closest friends from my Berkeley days went with the garin and lived their idealistic visions for several years. But eventually all but one family left Gezer; a few friends remained in Israel while others ended up back in the US, scattering into different professions and geographical locations. Despite the failure of our collective dream, we have remained a very close-knit group of friends, accompanying each other through joys and sorrows in lives now interlaced for fifty years.

JANUARY 9, 1972, AT THE WINGATE SPORTS INSTITUTE, IN THE TENT, RIGHT ON THE SEASHORE: RACHELI

Once again, I was writing at the seashore, a place that for me was especially romantic. I always wrote my most passionate letters in Hebrew, as I did this one:

I went down to the shore today – a few minutes after sunset. The sea elicits my longing, a sadness both quiet and sweet. And I want you so much, my beloved.

When the wind touches my face, I almost feel your hands caressing me.

I long to sit with you, close together, to softly sink into each other's eyes, into the blue of the sea, and delve into ourselves, into our shared depths. Do you understand it? Do you feel it?

I am moved, so moved by the tremendous power of the longing for you – against the backdrop of this beauty. You wrote to me that beauty arouses in you a certain kind of happiness that's also immersed in loneliness. Indeed. But this loneliness, in my imagination, is absent, and there is so much happiness.

I appended a cartoon I drew of myself while on the platoon's hike a week earlier. Decked out in my army fatigues with my rifle on my shoulder, I stopped the march to appreciate a narcissus.

David sent back his own, admittedly less artistic self-portrait:

JANUARY 18, 1972: RACHELI

Since I had so little free time during the NCO course, I began to sneak reading and writing letters during training sessions. That did make it seem rather like *Catch 22*: "It's so absurd to be writing you as I do right now – in a lesson learning how to write an official letter about military matters."

My letter was prompted by a letter I had received from Marcie, a close friend of David's in Berkeley, whom I had met and really liked, describing a severe depression she experienced after a break up with her boyfriend. I generalized and, therefore, agonized:

It worried me, this inability to face the complexity and pain. It also reminded me too much of what you wrote about your worries about academic life. I don't know - there seems to be some lack of roots in reality, some disconnection, or maybe not enough basic security for orientation, for the ability to see your way through (forgive the generalization) in American youth.

I felt that I was different, had "some kind of basic security in where I go," which I attributed to being a kibbutznik and an Israeli, having no inkling at the time that, after all, I would be the one who would deviate from the secure path I thought I was walking on.

JANUARY 20, 1972: DAVID

I wrote to report an amazing experience in the university library. I was supposed to be working on my research paper but, while killing time, I discovered a shelf with *yizker bikher*, memorial books for the destroyed Jewish communities of Eastern Europe, among them the book dedicated to my father's hometown in Poland, Wloclawek. There, I learned that after the ghetto was sealed off in 1941, a number of Jews were arrested for smuggling food. In the list of those shot for smuggling was Shimon Biezinski, who I assumed must have been a relative on my father's mother's side of the family. And, then, further down the list was the name Bialoglowsky, my grandfather's name!

What an incredible shock – I knew that my grandfather was killed by the Nazis (as was my grandmother), but I didn't know anything about the circumstances of his death. But here it was in front of my eyes, described in detail. It's things like this that make me very conscious that I'm a Jew; also conscious of how close I am to that destroyed Eastern European Jewish world and how shallow are my roots in America.

I learned much later that this was actually an error. In fact, my grandparents were deported to the Warsaw Ghetto and my grandfather died there in a typhus epidemic in the ghetto in December 1941. Racheli and I found his grave in the Warsaw Jewish cemetery many years later.

JANUARY 21, 1972: RACHELI:

Soon the sun will set. Sunsets should be shared, as should the flowers and the silent sadness within everything. I am visualizing you near, so near me. But sometimes it all seems like a tall tale or an animated movie with background music by Mozart. Sometimes I feel like I am watching myself, watching my "story" without the full echo that reverberates back, without the same dynamism, without the invisible threads of a glance, a movement, and being silent together. There was a time when the intellectual conversations we had were a kind of climax for me, a source of satisfaction, a vessel to drink from. Later, came the development of our emotions – our conversations about desires and fears, our examination of ourselves and our relationship.

Now I long for a shared togetherness without a sound, without words, without explanation and investigation. Closeness - close for the touch of my hand, so close that the warmth and softness that exudes out of me enters you without need of any bridging, without needing anything else.

JANUARY 24, 1971: RACHELI

Despite my wish for a simple, shared silence, I nevertheless returned to the more challenging question of our differing identities and their implications for a shared future. This was a hard nut to crack and I can still recall the angst I felt writing about it.

Maybe what I'm trying to ask of you is an honest analysis of your question – what is the part that I play in your feelings about Israel? I sometimes feel you're not clear about how you feel about my being an Israeli. I sometimes sense you try to deny my being a part of Israel. I recall a few times when you've said how untypical an Israeli, a kibbutznik you thought I was. There is a Galut in me too - galut from my identity. But the basic point of orientation is clear; I feel deeply secure about it. And it revolves around raising my children here. And if I didn't have that, I fear I'd be lost among my worries and dilemmas.

JANUARY 25, 1972: DAVID

The time was fast approaching to make concrete plans for my Pesach visit. We were determined not to let the mismatch between Racheli's three-week leave and my arrival around the time her leave was to end get in the way of our time together. We had already overcome the disappointment of the two earlier aborted visits and we were not going to let the Israeli army foil us again this time. I had relatives at Kibbutz Mishmar Ha-Emek, which was about a half an hour from Racheli's base, so I proposed to stay there when she had to be on duty. They would arrange for me to be a volunteer, which would entitle me to a small room (one of the old "Swedish Huts" that the kibbutz made available to temporary visitors) and to three meals a day. I was very fond of my father's cousin, Elisha, who was a real character - full of stories, very original opinions, an avid naturalist, a classical music and jazz enthusiast, and an Alexander practitioner. Racheli would hopefully be able to get off most evenings to come spend the night with me.

I actually had a place to stay closer to the base in Hadera with Aharon and Betta Schnitzer, two of my father's closest comrades from his Hashomer Hatzair group in Poland. But, as I wrote, "I have a very low tolerance for this guy – he is a 100% chauvinist. If I had to stay there for more than a few days, I'd go crazy." In the end, I stayed there for only *one* night ... and went crazy.

But, fantasies and plans aside, I was now deeply engaged in my research paper on Jewish intellectuals in Russia between the 1860s and the 1880s. It was for a seminar with the great Russian historian Martin Malia. I was reading Haskalah newspapers like *HaMagid*, written in the florid Hebrew that predated the development of Hebrew as a spoken language. It was tough sledding. The writers often used some clumsy fourteen-word phrase that we would express in two or three the words. Despite how long it took to decipher the language, I was finding some exciting things:

> *They have news articles and advertisements like modern newspapers, except they are from the shtetl, such as "Reb Cohen is selling his books – any buyers?" Also, some of the articles are ridiculous such as a child born in France with four eyes – two of them where his ears should be!*

Beyond these curiosities, though, was my discovery that the intellectuals I was studying had already turned away from assimilation into Russian culture and were floating Jewish nationalist ideas *before* the 1881 pogroms, not after, as most historians thought. What caused this development was their awareness of the rise of the new antisemitism in Germany in the 1870s. If Germany, which had recently emancipated the Jews, could harbor such racial hatred, what hope could there be for integration in Russia? Here's how I announced this discovery to the world:

> *I went to lunch on the terrace (you remember where we had lunch when you were in Berkeley?) and saw Fred Rosenbaum sitting there. I yelled: "Fred, I've just discovered a new theory of Jewish history." The whole terrace started laughing ... Maybe there's a future for me as an historian after all???*

JANUARY 28, 1972: DAVID

I was very pleased with the letters that I was receiving from Racheli:

I sense a new maturity and self-confidence. One thing neither of us probably realizes is how each of us has undoubtedly changed in the last year. I don't really feel it myself, but other people here have told me that it is true. I hope that we have both changed and matured in the same direction, so that when we are together, we will be even closer.

Meanwhile, in Berkeley, closer emotional ties were developing in the RJU. We had held a group reading of David Roskies' *Nightwords* midrash on the Holocaust:

The mood was very serious and very close. Afterwards, nobody wanted to leave the room. A friend of mine who was new to the group commented that he had never seen a campus group that exuded so much warmth and love as ours – a very unusual thing especially for a semi-political group.

I also reported on a letter from Shelly Schreter, my close friend who had left Berkeley the year before to start a doctorate at the London School of Economics, a degree he never finished. Shelly was intent on living in Israel and had just visited there, primarily in order to convince his wife Debbie, who had never been there, that they should make the move. While he didn't convey her reactions, I commented:

That is one of the problems with aliyah. One member of the couple wants to live there but the other doesn't. My parents are a good example: my father would love it, but my mother thinks it's ridiculous. I hope that Shelly doesn't have that problem.

Racheli and I would confront the same dilemma several times a few years later. Fortunately, we were able to come to a consensus between us, so that the ultimate decision to stay in the United States was not one-sided.

JANUARY 29, 1972: RACHELI

Departing this time from an ideological argument for kibbutz, I now wrote something much more quotidian about a weekend at home:

Today was a beautiful day. After a week of rain – a clean, fresh, sunny day.

Met two kids, puddle-hopping, covered with mud to their noses, still the smiles on their faces almost bursting out. I wanted you very much to be with me. I think probably because this is a part of my answer to the same questions about kibbutz and our future you've been asking.

Writing close to midnight, I ended with another poem by Leah Goldberg:

Night

A basket full of stars
The smell of whispering grasses.
Deep,
Deep within the dew,
Beats my heart.

Here are your footsteps approaching,
Scattering thousands of droplets.
Deep,
Deep within the dew,
Beats my heart.

FEBRUARY 1, 1972: DAVID

In response to Racheli's question about the part she played in my feelings about Israel, I reviewed some of my history:

The spring of 1970, when I was at Kibbutz Lahav, made me pessimistic about living on kibbutz. It was a bad experience [I

have no clear memory today of that being the case, but, rather,
the contrary]. Then, I went to Ulpan Akiva, which was good, but
not really Israel. And, then, when I spent the month of August with
you at Kfar Ruppin, my feelings really changed. And, of course, a
lot of that had to do with you, even though neither of us had the
courage to verbalize what we were beginning to feel.

There is no question that I am attracted to you because of certain
things you represent to me, but also because of things that are
unique to you. I really mean it when I say that you are a very,
very unusual person in my eyes.

"And in the end, the love you take is equal to the love you make." What
I really hope is that we will learn to love each other for the unique
individuals we are. I don't want to love Racheli the kibbutznik, the
corporal, the Israeli, but instead just Racheli – YOU.

FEBRUARY 2, 1972: DAVID

One of the characters in a novel of Joseph Hayim Brenner, the
great Hebrew writer of the Second Aliya, says: "The Temple was
destroyed two thousand years ago. Why are we still sitting in the
rubble playing with the stones?" I took this to be a critique of Jews
living in the Galut. Israelis need not ask the question, I thought,
perhaps because they were building a secular society with no need
for a Temple. But a Jew living outside of Israel has to constantly ask
Brenner's question if he or she is to remain Jewish.

In this sense, I feel closer to the Zionists of the first and second
aliya whom I'm reading about now – their tortured minds are
really not so different from my own, although their generation
was very different from mine in so many other ways.

But my view of Zionism was already out of date. What Brenner meant
by "playing in the rubble of the Temple" was two things: a religion
based on loss of sovereignty and exile, and religion altogether. He
and his generation rejected all religion in favor of a secular Hebrew
society. But after the Six Day War, religious Zionists sought to turn

Israel into a religious state in the biblical heartland of the West Bank. And some extremists even wanted to rebuild the actual Third Temple.

FEBRUARY 4, 1972: DAVID

Just over a month until we would finally be together and my thoughts, like Racheli's, repeatedly turned to the Song of Songs. I transcribed a long passage from chapter five of the biblical love poem and added:

> *In Shir Ha'shirim, the beloved comes to the locked garden of his beloved and she lets him in. Perhaps she is afraid and it is the first time she has opened herself. But she does it because otherwise her love would never be fulfilled. But then her beloved disappears and the love never reaches its climax.*
>
> *I hope that is not this way with us – and that even though I will be gone a month after I arrive, we will come to fulfillment. This year of letters has been like one arousing, agonizing caress after another.*

FEBRUARY 8, 1972: RACHELI

With my excited anticipation of David's visit, I was also – frankly – scared. We had started writing explicitly about our hopes to have sex when he came. This meant I had to make plans for birth control, something I knew enough about in theory, but zero in practice. I would need to have a visit with an OB-GYN, not a simple matter as a kibbutz girl. I would have to ask the kibbutz nurse to set up an appointment for me at the central health clinic in Afula – terribly embarrassing! -- and then get a day's leave from the army to go to the appointment, without revealing what it was for.

I chose the easy way out: I left a note for my mother – to be opened after I had left home from a weekend leave – using the excuse of being in the army to ask *her* to talk to the kibbutz nurse and get me the appointment. In hindsight, I don't know why it didn't occur to me that the army infirmary at Machane Shmonim dispensed birth control! I am sure it did so in spades, after all, the Israeli army in general, and the base in particular, were co-ed and offered plenty of opportunities for sexual activity, even as that was officially, of course, forbidden while on duty.

Upon completing the NCO course, I sent David a picture of myself after receiving my promotion.

I now had a three-week vacation after the completion of the course, a vacation that I had hoped in vain to spend with David. But there were some compensations. One of the greatest pleasures of my leave was hikes in the hills surrounding Kfar Ruppin, pursuing, as ever, my love affair with anemones.

We found a small hill, the hillside was green with a few small, light-colored flowers. We climbed up on it and suddenly – such bright, fiery red! like a beam of light bursting out of the green. It literally seized your eyes. There is some kind of magic spell in the anemones: you can't take your eyes off of them. Your eyes just gulp down the bright spots – and are not satiated. Each red anemone is such a new surprise of perfection, richness and vitality.

My David – that is exactly the moment, the place within our dreams.

FEBRUARY 9, 1972: DAVID

I received a letter written on January 21; in other words, it took *nineteen days* to arrive. I had a theory of why:

Evidently the censor, who finally opened a letter, was so entranced by what you had to say that he just couldn't send it on (I'm worried that some censor may have fallen in love with you after reading your letters – I know that if I were the censor, I would).

Racheli had written this particular letter in beautiful Hebrew: maybe that's why the censor finally decided to do his job. She claimed that she didn't have a poet's sensitivity for words, but this letter proved otherwise: "have I ever told you how much I admire your artistic creativity – in words and drawing?" In later years, Racheli would write and illuminate Jewish marriage contracts (*ketubot*) and other works of art. And she would also write a very original and eloquent memoir of her kibbutz childhood.

FEBRUARY 15-16, 1972 [IN HEBREW ON AMERICAN AIRLINES STATIONERY]: DAVID
ALTITUDE: HIGH
LOCATION: DIRECTLY OVER NOWHERE

I was returning from a five-day trip to New York for a conference of Young Judaea (surprisingly, I have no memory today of attending this conference or even of the New York trip altogether). According to this letter, I flew "illegally" on a youth fare, which applied to those 21 and younger and I was now an "old man" of 22. I had borrowed somebody's ID card, faked his signature and passed myself off as him, evidently inspired by my successful subterfuge in evading the American army. I find it hard to believe today that I actually did this and that it left no lasting impression.

As to the conference, I was unimpressed by the Young Judaea leadership and the low intellectual level of the movement. Not my cup of tea. But I made some new friends and got together with Noam Sachs, my co-counselor from the previous summer. And I haunted the New York bookstores, buying up a lot of books in Jewish Studies of the sort unavailable in Berkeley.

Back in Berkeley, I would now have to focus like a laser on my research seminar paper since I had less than a month to finish it. Independently of the Hebrew sources I was using, I had also been reading the biblical scholar Yehezkel Kaufmann's great work, *Golah ve-Nekhar* (Exile and Estrangement). I thought I could apply his argument that Jewish nationalism did not represent a continuation of Jewish messianic movements:

> *Kaufman says that Jewish nationalism is a continuation of the quest of assimilationist emancipation's desire to 'acquire' a homeland. Frustrated by the failure of emancipation, the Haskalah turned to regions outside of Europe to fulfill its goals.*

FEBRUARY 19, 1972: DAVID

"Dear pen-pal, in exactly three weeks I will get on a plane to London." I was torn between two conflicting emotions: for the time to go faster so that I could already be in Israel and for the time to slow down so that I could get my academic work done. Meanwhile, in Berkeley:

> *Now is one of the nicest times of year. Winter is not exactly over but spring is trying hard to push it out. The cherry trees are in bloom everywhere in Berkeley and everywhere you walk, their pink flowers fill the air with a soft, sweet smell. Last night, before Havdalah, we sat outside watching the sunset and feeling like as long as there is spring, life is really worth living.*

February in Berkeley is still our favorite month, when the flowering trees first burst into bloom.

FEBRUARY 22, 1972: DAVID

Our letters had come to a kind of plateau or even dead end. We had developed our relationship as far as it could go – or so it seemed to me – in writing and now we could only mark time until our long-delayed reunion: "You are right – we will know what will happen by how my hand feels in yours, and how yours feels in mine." In anticipation of that meeting, I got a haircut: "Prepare yourself: we are going to be twins. Elaine Schlackman [one of my friends from the Radical Jewish Union] just cut my hair and she did it exactly like your hair, at least the way it is in the picture you sent me when you were drafted." We would now both have the then-very fashionable "Afros."

FEBRUARY 27 – MARCH 1, 1972: RACHELI

I feel like I'm holding my breath - waiting for you to come. I sit in my room, alone, trying very hard to find the words to tell you how much I miss you. How beautiful I'm sure it will be when we are together. You know – it's only two weeks from tomorrow.

There really was nothing more to say, but since our letters were such a lifeline for both of us, we kept writing:

When I see an almond tree blooming – a white cloud hanging over a shining red field of anemones -- it is simple and true and beautiful. David – it will be that way for us when we are together. I'm sure. It has to – we have been waiting, building, hoping for this over a year now.

Berkeley and Israel were on the same seasonal clock as flowering trees in both places bloomed simultaneously. We were such romantics that, despite being corny, we seemed to both cheer up when we wrote each other lines of this sort. The next day I fell back on surer ground: the words of a true poet, Yehuda Amichai: "All the miracles of the Bible and all the fairy tales/ happened between us when we were together." My commentary was brief: "I hope so – for us."

A little while back, David had written me that his parents were coming to Jerusalem for a one-semester sabbatical and would, in fact, already be there by the time he arrived. So, we had to plan both visiting them in Jerusalem and also having them come to Kfar Ruppin for the kibbutz Passover Seder, which was an elaborate affair with the whole kibbutz plus every family hosting at least five or six guests, the kibbutz's choir singing all the Haggadah songs, and enough matzah balls to feed 500 hungry mouths.

MARCH 2, 1972: DAVID [IN HEBREW]

Muki Tsur [the kibbutz emissary who visited Berkeley in the fall of 1970] is staying with me and, since he is asleep now, I won't type on the typewriter. Muki is so charming and, besides that, he's really brilliant. We've already talked about many topics and he has many opinions and thoughts that are very original and interesting. Nu, so it turns out that there are, after all, Israelis one can learn from! Muki is just now finishing a book about the sources and history of the kibbutz. He told me that people will kill him in Israel once the book comes out. "Why?" I asked. It turns out that he reveals all kinds of strange episodes in the history, which people never talk about, for example, there is a chapter in the book about suicides on the kibbutz.

MARCH 4, 1972: DAVID

I had had a long conversation with Muki about my research paper and he offered some excellent criticisms. Most importantly, we argued about it in Hebrew:

I suddenly felt how much I wanted to be in Israel. Then, I got a wonderful letter from you and for a precious moment, I was out of Berkeley and in a beautiful world of springtime with you. It was only a year since you were here. What a long time ago it was! I remember how I tried to kiss you good night and you got embarrassed, so I kissed you on the cheek. Racheli, you were really a little girl then, but now your letters are so different. I somehow feel that the Racheli who will be waiting for me at the airport when I get off the plane will be a woman.

Imagination was now about to meet reality:

Love is so much in dreams meeting bodies, intertwining until you can't tell them apart. Dreams: laughing together a lot – walking together silently hand-in-hand. Lying next to each other in the cool silence of morning, embracing in the soft smell of your skin, bodies entangled in oneness, never wanting to let go, watching the sun play with your hair and my future.

MARCH 5, 1972: DAVID

I've written 27 pages of my paper – it will probably be at least 45 pages (yech – it's supposed to be 30 but I always did have a big mouth and lots of hot air). I'm supposed to present an oral report (if I keep sitting at this desk, it will turn into an <u>anal</u> report).

The next day was Purim and I was unlikely to get much work done that evening because we had convinced the Berkeley police to close off my one-block street, "for a Purim riot." We posted signs all over town, crafted by Bradley Burston, the creative impresario of the RJU: "Jews to the streets!" The plan was to start at the Hillel House on Bancroft Avenue, process with groggers down to Atherton Street and then hold a drunken "riot" in front of my window. It succeeded beyond our expectations and many joined us as we passed them on the street.

MARCH 8, 1972: RACHELI:

We were nearing the point where my letters would no longer reach David. He was stopping in London for a few days and would be heading eastward, towards Israel, faster than my letters could travel westward. I didn't mind that much. Writing letters daily had become "somehow like writing some kind of a diary." Clearly, I was writing mostly for myself, to put on paper the feelings that were exploding inside me: "David, I can't wait for that moment when all the words with which we filled the spaces between us with will not be needed, replaced by 'being' together – tenderly, beautifully. I hope more so than in my dreams."

And, so, it would come to pass.

DAVID

I walked out the sliding door at the Lod Airport and Racheli jumped into my arms. I can still remember that embrace. My parents, who were spending the spring in Israel, had met her at the airport before my arrival. She had to come directly from Machane Shmonim in her uniform since there was a swearing-in ceremony there earlier that day. We drove together to Jerusalem, where we stayed in the apartment my parents had rented on Radak Street. To their eternal credit and without any sign of awkwardness, they set us up on a double bed (actually a fold-out couch) in the living room. The next day, we all drove up the Jordan Valley, which was brilliantly green from the winter rains and the slopes covered with fields of red anemones.

We had spilled so much ink and worn out so many typewriter ribbons preparing for a sexual relationship, that you might wonder how that went. On our first two nights, too much anxiety

Two Afros in love: picture taken David's father in
Jerusalem, the day after his arrival in Israel

accompanied our passion. But we had so much confidence in each
other that we did not lose heart. On Shabbat morning, after our
second night together, we overcame our inhibitions and, from that
moment on, nothing could stop us.

We have only two written documents from the three and a half
weeks I was in Israel. The first is an undated, handwritten letter
that I evidently wrote on Sunday evening, March 19, after that first
weekend together and when Racheli had already returned to her
army base.

My dearest love,

I suddenly miss you very, very much. I've been reading Saul
Bellow's Herzog and I just came across a passage which moved
me very much:

"And then he [Father Herzog] died. And that vivid blood of his
turned to soil, in all the shrunken passages of his body. And
there the body, too -- ah, God! – wastes away; and leaves its
bones, and even the bones at last wear away and crumble to

dust in that shallow place of deposit. And thus humanized, this planet in its galaxy of stars and worlds goes from void to void, infinitesimal, aching with its unrelated significance. Unrelated?

Herzog, with one of his Jewish shrugs, whispered, "Nu, meile..."

I don't know, somehow at this time, when I feel as if my life is starting all over again, as if I am being born again through our love – all this incredible happiness brings terrible thoughts of life's end. And I think about the people I love and how much it matters not to take them for granted, not to allow the most important relationships to be based only on everyday trivialities. And most of all, please, please, love me "with all your heart, all your spirit, and all your might."

Please don't think I'm sad or depressed, on the contrary. I felt this weekend so much love for you that I can't express it. I think it's a miracle [in Hebrew] "And who can look at the face of God?" Maybe that's why it's so hard to put in words. And maybe when you feel yourself confronting one of the miracles and mysteries of life, you cannot avoid confronting all the others.

This is the sort of letter that you write and throw away. But I think that I will send it anyway. We've long since passed refraining from saying things to each other. For better or worse, you have to live with all of my crazy emotions. And it makes me so happy that you want to. Strange sort of love letter – better stop before it really gets out of hand.

I love you, Your David

The second is a note in Hebrew attached to the door of the room where I was staying in Kibbutz Mishmar Ha-Emek:

For any interested female soldier –

I am in Elisha Amir's room (the last row of houses up the hill) or in the dining room.

Please pop over there because I really, really miss you.

[in English] You-know-who

It was in Mishmar Ha-Emek that month that I gave Racheli the nickname that has stuck to this day. Once, when she arrived in the evening after hitchhiking from her base, her uniform totally disheveled, I mobilized a Hebrew slang word I had learned: *mechukmeket*, which can be applied to someone whose appearance is messed-up, in this case "unmilitary."

A few months later at Mitzpe Shalem... still "mechukmeket." With time, that overly-lengthy word got truncated and became "Chuki."

RACHELI

I do remember that "mechukmeket" evening vaguely: I had had a day of endless chores and duties and when I was finally done, I didn't want to waste the ten minutes it would take to shower at the base. So, I ran to catch a late-evening bus. Soon after being dubbed "Chuki," I had to reciprocate and crowned David "Dubcek." I don't remember why I named him after the Czech leader of the Prague Spring, whom my family, indeed, admired, but who had nothing to do with David. Soon, however, I added "Vavooki" (inspired by Wloclawek, his father's home town). Both of them stuck.

These endearments are just the little signs of how wonderfully our time together went. Everything we had agonized about in our letters melted away and the challenges of shuttling between my army base and Mishmar Ha-Emek paled in comparison to the magic of being together.

As I had hoped, I was able to get off at least three evenings a week. Several times I had a trusty companion, Nili, who was from Mishmar Ha-Emek and tagged along with me to see her family there. We were quite friendly anyway, being both hardy, no-nonsense type of girls. She, however, was revealed to be truly courageous several years later. While hitchhiking at the same junction to Mishmar Ha-Emek, she was picked up by a car that turned out to be driven by Palestinian terrorists. They intended to abduct her and then. . . God knows what. When she realized what was going on, she opened the door of the speeding car and jumped out. She suffered major injuries and it took a very long course for her to recover. But she was remarkably resilient and overcame these, only to fall back on the same inner strength to fight cancer later on. I would make sure to see her every time we visited Elisha's family for decades thereafter.

We were so drunk on our love and didn't let any obstacles get in our way. For most of one week, I was in another one of those field trainings in the sand dunes near the seashore. I arranged with David for him to take the Afula-to-Tel Aviv bus in the evening and I would stand by the roadside to flag the bus down. It worked! I snuck him into my pup tent. We delighted in being together until it became evident that his giddiness was not because, as the Song of Songs says "I am love-sick," but because of a high fever from being virus-sick. Out of the encampment we went, back to the main road where we flagged down a car (with me in uniform, it was easy to hitchhike) and he got a ride to nearby Kibbutz Ein Ha-Horesh to recuperate with relatives.

Our time in Kfar Ruppin was, of course, the most important. To be there together as a couple, in the presence of my family, my classmates and, frankly, the whole kibbutz, was a public declaration. And, of course, we got to take those walks in the hills and fields surrounding the kibbutz that I had dreamed of and to visit all my wildflower friends. We also took a magical day-hike in Wadi Amud, a wild ravine meandering from the Galilee mountains to the Sea of Galilee, with David's Berkeley friends, Sherman and Melodie, our "unintentional matchmaker" Navah, and my soul-mate friend, Devorale. The wadi was bursting with flowers. Water cascaded in rivulets and collected in large puddles, which we traversed by a combination of wide jumps and precarious balancing on rocks. It was a way of bringing our worlds closer together, starting to build a shared whole. We would need to preserve the magic of the visit for an additional five months of letter writing, but it would be so much easier now that we had a real relationship, a true love.

In the fields of Kfar Ruppin

ON OUR WAY
April-July 1972

APRIL 8, 1972, WRITTEN IN LOD AIRPORT, MAILED FROM LONDON [IN HEBREW]: DAVID

"Goodbyes" are hard not only because you physically leave somebody you love, but also because it suddenly makes you aware of how fluid time is. When you say goodbye and end a good period, then it makes you realize how temporary everything is in this world. That realization sometimes causes the greatest feelings of loneliness. But I think that what was good about the last 3 weeks was that we somehow managed to conquer time, to make it go slower, to appreciate every moment. Maybe only love can do that (I always said I was a romantic) – and maybe that explains why I don't feel unhappy now.

As I said to you, I never really said "I love you" to any girl before. I still don't quite believe that it really happened and that it felt so natural.

APRIL 8, 1972: RACHELI

David flew off to London on April 8 and, before the day ended, I went back to our letter writing as did he, as I would learn a week or so later when I got his letter posted in London. The transition back was hard: "Suddenly – again that boundless distance, and I am talking into a silence." In light of the voluminous correspondence we immediately resumed, it is funny that I chose this analogy: "from the moment you left I feel like I've been emptied out, like a pen that has run out of ink – actually, even more abruptly." Yet my pen certainly kept on flowing and we accelerated our letter-writing, sending a letter almost every day.

Even though I anticipated having a very hard time being apart and waiting for David's return in the fall, I now felt completely sure of our love and of our success in translating the endless longing and worries into a beautiful sexual and sensual union.

I feel somehow filled up completely with our experience together and completely taken by my feelings for you. Before, there was doubt and worry, and sometimes the feeling that all was just fantasy – going nowhere. I have no way to say this but to say that now I'm in the peace of emunah shlemah [perfect faith].

The next day I was smack back in the reality of army life, writing a letter while "sitting in a tent out in the field, rather than at the base, freezing in my soaking wet clothes, waiting for a miracle to get me out of here." I consoled myself by pouring out my longing:

I wish to hold out my hand and very slightly touch your face, feel your forehead and follow the soft line of your eyebrows, down your cheek – I'll touch your warm lips. Gently, my love, I wish to kiss you.

But I could not write such passionate lines for long. I was exhausted from the day in the rain and the next morning we were to get up at 4:00 AM to hike to the beach for "the absolutely last live fire target practice in my history, I HOPE!"

This time, I was the supervising NCO of my troop of girls, about to complete their basic training. It was much scarier than doing the shooting myself, since we, commanders, were terrified that one of the girls would accidentally shoot one of us. A story circulated among us of a recruit whose Uzi submachine gun had jammed. Rather than laying it down on the ground and calling the commander over, she turned around with it to face the NCO, who was standing right behind her. Pointing the gun at the NCO she said: "It won't shoot" and demonstrated by squeezing the trigger. It did shoot. This was probably apocryphal, a didactic story meant to assure we would proceed with great caution. We repeated the story to our recruits and, as they lay down with their guns to start the target shooting, we yelled at the top of our voices: "Stay lying down! No matter what, NEVER turn around!" We were all greatly relieved when it ended and we were all safe and sound.

But there were also some moments of fun and levity. During our week of field training, we managed to go swimming in the sea in our underwear, since we certainly had not packed bathing suits. We lay on the beach and got a nice tan. There was also an adventure I relayed in detail, relishing reliving it:

I went on leave with another girl to Hadera to watch Midnight Cowboy, which I thought was rather good. After the show we went to the bathroom and, while we were there, suddenly the lights went off. Suspicious. We went to the main door – locked! Went to all other possible doors and entrances - all closed and locked; all but two windows. Went to the window and yelled out to the street for help. Nobody there: everybody goes to sleep in Hadera at 8:30 pm. The window was 6 meters above the ground. The only hope left – the other window. And, to our surprise and delight, we found a ladder leaning on the outside wall under the window. We managed to get it standing up with the help of the IDF (some bored soldier that was walking down the street and was very happy to help two "fellow-women"); finally made it down to the ground and freedom!

To end the successful rescue nicely, we got a ride to the Field Training with a nice guy who also invited us for "midnight coffee" at a restaurant. . . on our way (a little off it, really) to the training.

At the Field Training

Meanwhile, I was also beginning my long saga of wiggling my way out of officers' training. I knew that, given my record in the pre-draft aptitude tests, being selected as the "outstanding cadet" in basic training, and my performance as an NCO, I was bound to be invited to try out for this course. And it was not an invitation you could easily turn down. In hindsight, I cannot reconstruct what the predominant reason was, but I did have a list. Becoming an officer would entail spending considerably more time at Machane Shmonim, probably doing at least two tours of duty as a commander of a company of new recruits and then as an officer in the NCO course. It also meant I'd have to consent, which was not really a free choice, to serve an extra four months in the army. Perhaps more important than these practical considerations was the anti-militaristic stance I had been cultivating, much influenced by David, the Jewish Radical, and, of course, *Catch 22*. I was rather out of sync with my army colleagues and kibbutz cohort, perhaps not fully aware that I had started a process of assimilation into American Jewish culture.

SUNDAY, APRIL 16, 1972: DAVID (BACK IN BERKELEY)

When I walked into my room last week, I noticed something incredible. This vine that had been growing outside my window somehow grew between the window panes and is now growing inside my room. It is very strange and very beautiful, it's nice to have the out-of-doors growing inside, just like it's nice to feel that you are here even though you are there.

I was now facing nearly five months until I would be able to return to Israel for the 1972-73 academic year, when I planned to enroll as a visiting graduate student at the Hebrew University. After completing my master's degree in June, I was to go to the Goethe Institute in Germany to learn German, finally arriving in Israel in early September.

APRIL 17, 1972: RACHELI

I got your letters from London and L.A. yesterday. They were amazing – one, because I realized how any kind of connection with you – even a word – makes me so completely happy. And the other thing is, finding out we were writing each other almost the same things. I found your letters saying almost exactly what I was trying to explain and tell you in my letters.

Writing all these pages is really just an excuse for saying – I love you. You know, had it not looked silly and ridiculous, I would have filled up all these pages with just that.

APRIL 18, 1972: DAVID

Racheli, my love, I think that during our three weeks together, I felt more alive and complete than ever before. Somehow, all the magic eternity that echoes in the memories of childhood came back. I think of the organ concert that we heard in the Old City of Jerusalem – I felt a sense of beauty that I couldn't have without you.

But I couldn't spend all my time writing love letters. My main academic task for the next two months was to prepare for and take the master's exam in modern European history. This would mean cramming dozens of books. And the political atmosphere was also heating up: Nixon had bombed North Vietnam and there was increasing unrest on campus. It would be hard to avoid that, even if I was meant to keep my nose firmly planted in books. The Radical Jewish Union was continuing its activities as well. A "big shot" from the Ichud kibbutz movement (the movement Kfar Ruppin belonged to), Meir Zarmy ("it sounds like Meir's army") was coming to Berkeley because "he wants to meet some Radical Jewish Students (capital letters, please) and we will oblige by asking him some sticky questions about why the Ichud wants to settle in Gaza, etc." Later, Racheli wrote that Zarmy's daughter, Yael, had been in her NCO training course. Small world. Too bad I didn't know that at the time.

APRIL 19, 1972: RACHELI

At my next leave home, David's absence was palpable, much more intense than in the army barracks or pup tents.

Sitting in my room, alone in bed. I miss you here more than I do in the army. Somehow, being alone there seems more natural, or rather, it fits into the abnormality of life in the army.

But being in bed now – where there used to be a crack [to make a double bed we put together two single beds and mattresses: there was always a crack in the middle, where you got stuck if you weren't careful – this became a standing joke between us] there's just the edge of the bed, makes me feel lonely. Makes me realize how much I want you. It's so hard to drop back to no sexual relationship and have it all withdrawn into memory and desire. It's like replacing a field of blooming anemones by a dried flower, reminding you of the last spring, promising the coming one.

I was home for a week on a special leave granted by the army to study for my last matriculation exam in geography. But I didn't spend much time perusing my books. Instead, I went for walks in the hills and fields surrounding the kibbutz, which were particularly beautiful just then. I did take the exam and got a decent grade, so I guess some brain space was reserved for that, even though it didn't feel like it at the time.

APRIL 26, 1972: DAVID

My visit to Israel had unleashed a new eroticism in our relationship that, at a distance of 10,000 miles, we tried to recapture in words:

I miss making love with you as much as you. I miss kissing you and feeling your tongue send shivers down my spine. I miss touching your body and feeling it respond and feeling your hands on my skin making me want you so much. I miss the breathless feeling inside you, becoming one. And I miss the quiet moments after making love when no words are needed – just to hold each other, knowing that all the words have been said by our bodies.

Not all of our letters were consumed by such overheated passion. I was also buoyed by my academic work:

Last night I spent four hours talking to a very bright friend of mine from the history department about all sorts of problems in modern European history. I had this tremendous feeling of intellectual excitement. I left his house with about eight books and a feeling that I was going to win this game of the master's exam. It's at moments like these that I really think that my destiny is to be a professor of history.

On the other hand, serving as a teaching assistant for Professor Webster's Modern Jewish History class was less than uplifting. He used big words in his lectures that made the students laugh when they couldn't understand him. Their ignorance was breathtaking: when Webster mentioned the prophet Ezekiel, one student wanted to know how to spell it and whether the book was in the library. In addition; "I held office hours for the first time, so I finally made it from student to teacher. But nobody came to see my moment of glory except for a friend of mine. So much for my role as a university teacher."

APRIL 26, 1972: RACHELI

As soon as he got home to Berkeley, David developed his photos from the visit and sent me copies. I received them on April 26 and they helped a lot in reliving the joy of our time together and lifting the cloud of my loneliness: "I keep looking at the pictures - especially the one taken near your parents' house, of the two of us with the Afros. I see it, and many of my friends here who saw it see some kind of glow over us – together."

But words were still the main avenue we had for reaching each other, and I felt that they failed me:

They don't hold within them the warmth of a kiss, they don't hold within them the softness of a hand caressing, they don't hold in them the light in your eyes when we are together. . . the magical quiet when I lie next to you, and the way the warmth and beauty within you streams into me, fills me and overruns the banks, and floods me with happiness. A great happiness, and a purity that shines - and a sense of peace in our togetherness.

Sometimes I feel like all of me is overrun with longing, that there is nothing left inside me except for the pining. There is a great pull towards a point at an infinite distance, toward you. I am all desire for you, literally "my soul thirsts for you, my flesh longs for you [Psalms 63:2]"

I have never loved like this before – and it's so good – good without end.

APRIL 29, 1972: DAVID

Letters no longer seemed sufficient and we were both desperate to hear each other's voices. But international calls of the duration that would satisfy were prohibitively expensive. The solution? Someone I knew had figured out the dial tones that the phone company used for each number (this was still in the days of rotary phones but the international phone system used the tones that would become familiar from the later "touch tone" phones). He made me a cassette tape with the phone number for Kfar Ruppin. I had used it a few times, although I'm not sure that I ever succeeded in connecting that way with Racheli; the closest I got was her brother. Then I tried again, addressed the person on the other end in my best Hebrew – and got a response in ...Portuguese! The tape had evidently stretched a tiny bit and dialed not just the wrong number, but the wrong country. That was the end of that particular (illegal) escapade.

APRIL 29, 1972: DAVID

Racheli was now determined to avoid becoming an officer. I asked: Was she opposed to the course itself or to what she might have to do as an officer? Or was it a principled stand against de facto acceptance of what the army stood for? Then again, if she was going to have to train soldiers in Machane Shmonim anyway, maybe it would be better to do so as an officer? "After-thought: does it help to have me give my two-cents worth or would you prefer me to keep my mouth shut?" However, I did have some "useful" advice for her geography matriculation exam:

> Good luck ... as long as you can tell them where Berkeley, Calif. is, you should be all right. Remember that Mississippi has 4 s's, 4 i's and 2 p's. And also it helps to remember that the earth is round (and so are stars). Furthermore, rumor has it that the sun rises in the east and sets in the west, but that's only a rumor. Lucky for you that you will have already taken the test before you get this advice.

APRIL 30 – MAY 2, 1972: RACHELI

My report from the military front:

> Tomorrow morning, we go for a day's hike (35 kilometers) 20 miles to the Dotan Valley [in the West Bank, where my brother Gil had fought during the Six Day War], where the recruits get their Nachal insignia. I won't get mail. I won't be able to write tomorrow. "Duty calls for sacrifice" (Hah!).

As for Officers' Course. . . I'm taking the tests Wednesday. . . and then I plan to see CATCH 22!

The tests have one day of written exams (I.Q. and so on) that are very hard to fool the testers on. The second day has all kinds of personality tests based on acting in a group formed for that purpose that has to fulfill all kinds of tasks. At least there I can be sure to be showing "no motivation."

While I was still unsure if I could worm my way out of officers training, I continued to lobby to get posted to a Nachal settlement as soon as possible. I hoped a middle ground between my wishes and the army's needs would allow me to stay true to my emerging political consciousness. I wanted to be reasonably close to Jerusalem so I could visit David easily. Ideally, the settlement would be on an Egged bus line route. I did not want to serve in a settlement established on land previously inhabited or cultivated by Palestinians, nor adjacent to a Palestinian refugee camp or village. That left a few settlements in the Jordan Valley that I was sure – naively so in nearly fifty years' hindsight – would soon be returned to Jordan in a comprehensive peace deal (an independent Palestinian state in the West Bank and Gaza was not on the horizon yet).

The political awakening that led to my position also involved rethinking the status of Palestinians within Israel of the 1967 borders, whom we referred to as "Israeli Arabs," an unconscious erasure of their Palestinian identity. In this context, I relayed an important conversation with a girl who shared my tent. She was from a Hashomer Hatzair kibbutz called Bar'am on the Lebanon border. In light of that movement's public opposition to settlements on Palestinian land in the Gaza strip, I wondered: did her fellow members discuss their own difficult history?

Kibbutz Bar'am was situated right next to the ruins of Ikrit and Biram, two Palestinian villages whose inhabitants were expelled during the 1948 war. Most of the population fled to Lebanon, where they settled in the Palestinian refugee camps, which eventually became sprawling, crowded and impoverished towns, but some resettled in a large village within Israel, hoping that the IDF would keep its promise to allow them to return. In 1951, the Israeli Supreme Court ruled in their favor, ordering a repatriation. Days before the ruling was to take effect the IDF demolished all the remaining buildings in the two villages and blocked their return. In the early 1970s, the villagers staged sit-ins in the ruined villages and the issue was very hotly debated then.

My tent-mate said that, indeed, the kibbutz members often discussed this issue and had even published a booklet of opinion pieces by members, but only for internal consumption, keeping it very much hidden from public view. It was important to me to learn that it was discussed but I felt like the discussion was futile, as it led to no open public reckoning. It was becoming harder and harder to swallow the heroic story I was raised on, in which we, Israeli Jews fighting for our very survival, were always on the side of justice.

MAY 2, 1972: DAVID

My progress on preparing for the master's examination was slow. I now had only two weeks to go. Here was my daily study schedule:

I wake up, fool around and wander over to campus to read for an hour. Have lunch with my friends for two hours. Read another hour; wander home to see if there's a letter from you. Read an hour or two in the evening. In short, I'm afflicted with the dreaded disease of LAZINESS. . . At night I keep dreaming about such important and famous questions as: why did the German Social Democrats become bourgeois and is liberalism a precondition for fascism?

MAY 5, 1972, 1:30 AM: DAVID

Just when everything about the summer had been decided and I was about to send in my money for the German language course, I suddenly changed my mind: I would not go to Germany, after all, but instead come to Israel in July! I couldn't wait until morning to write. How had I imagined that I could wait until the fall? Rather, I would fly to London after finishing the spring quarter, tour a bit in Europe, meeting up with my parents who would be on their way back from Israel and then take the boat from Athens to Haifa in early July. I asked my father to try to get a hold of Racheli by phone at Kfar Ruppin to tell her the news. He did.

MAY 9, 1972 (?): RACHELI

Good news!!! No more problem with Officers' Course!

I went to take the tests on Wed. After writing three tests we had this questionnaire to fill out for Intelligence (making sure there is no spy or any such thing in the family). I had to sign a statement saying I'm a candidate for Officers' Course. I raised my hand and asked whether a person who refuses to go to the course had to sign that, too. I got thrown out of class.

The girl who was giving us the tests was rather dumb. She started screaming at me for asking that question. She wanted to know WHY I asked that question. I told her it was just because I wanted to know the answer. I scared her a little bit by telling her in a very angry tone how it was her duty to give all the information I ask for and so on. She let me go back into the class. I said, "Thank you, but I still wish to know the answer to my question." Then she got mad again – why didn't I sign a waiver form before taking the tests.? I gave it to her again for not giving us any information about that new discovery.

So – she told me to go sign that form in the office. I went to the office and signed this form saying I give away my right to take tests.

Then I had an interview with the head officer in charge of the Officers' Testing. He was about 50-years old and very fatherly. We talked for a while about the subject and other things. And – I managed to convince him there's no chance that I'll go to the course: I don't want to be an officer and thus, there's no sense in taking the tests. He accepted my waiver and – sent me home!

Free!

I was thrilled with this turn of events and wanted to celebrate my freedom with someone, but there was no one to do it with: all my NCO friends were taking the tests and very eager to pass them successfully. I had enough sense to know not to draw them into my little freedom dance. I went back to Machane Shmonim and reported to the commanding officer about my escapade. She was not amused but there was nothing she could do – I'd been kicked out and the train had left the station. I did not worry that she might retaliate by keeping me at the base because I knew we were going to get our postings the next day, so that train had already left the station too.

To further entertain David and show him I hadn't been reading the subversive literature he'd recommended in vain (*Catch 22* and *Slaughterhouse Five*), I recounted some of my "work" during the tests:

Of course, the tests were easy and boring. I tried to put some jokes into them. For example – we had to write up stories corresponding to pictures. One picture was very unclear – I thought I saw a bridge and rocks and cliffs behind it. My story opened in a very dramatic scene. Two guys have been sitting near the bridge all day waiting for the friend who had disappeared mysteriously in the early hours of a foggy morning. There has been no sign of him. It was getting near dark. What has happened to him? Will he come back, ever? Well, it turns out that fellow had been lying down behind a rock on the other side of the bridge all day – reading "Everything You Wanted to Know about Sex but Were Afraid to Ask!"

In hindsight, it seems the army did well to kick me out of the officers' course.

MAY 8, 1972: DAVID

In the midst of my joy at accelerating my arrival in Israel came stunning political news: President Nixon announced a blockade of North Vietnam, which seemed to escalate the war that we had fought against for so long. I described my feelings as resurrecting how I felt in October 1962, less than a decade earlier, during the Cuban Missile Crisis. I remembered feeling this awful sense that the world could be destroyed and that I had no control over what might happen. Now, it felt as if we were captives of a madman in Washington. Who knew that this madness fifty years later would seem all-too-tame?

But we refused to be passive:

At 10:00 pm, I was sitting in my room reading, when I heard a large crowd outside, yelling. I ran downstairs and found thousands of people demonstrating against the war. The demonstration turned into a full-fledged riot: windows smashed, policemen attacked and attacking, fires set in the street, barricades built. I must confess something terrible: I don't think I am a violent person, but I felt such rage that I threw several rocks at police cars. It was as if a terrible feeling of impotence had overtaken me so that the only way to avoid going crazy was to strike out and DO SOMETHING ...

We often talk about why didn't the Jews protest against the Nazis during World War II? Why didn't they resist? Why were people in Germany silent? Sometimes, when I find it hard to believe that Hitler really existed and the Nazis really did what they did, I think about what the US is doing now and even though it is hardly on the same scale as the Nazis, I realize that governments are capable of anything. Putting past and present together, there doesn't seem to be any choice but to be an anarchist, n'est-ce pas?

Of course, I understood that the situations were hardly comparable and that resistance against the Nazis meant certain death, while the worst that could happen to us was to get arrested. I didn't write in the letter that I escaped this fate by diving under a car in a parking building as the police circled around looking for demonstrators. I was proud of the fact that we refused to remain silent, even though the protest was ineffectual.

MAY 10, 1972: RACHELI

To celebrate the end of commanding basic training, we had a

kumzitz campfire on the beach. That was, I am sure, great fun, but "I left in the middle. I can't enjoy myself. I get very lonely and miss you very much. I prefer to be alone in my room but somehow be with you by writing to you, imagining you next to me." On lucky nights, sleep was even better than writing or reading letters: "When I dream of you, I find myself disappointed after I wake up because what has been very real, vanishes. But, on the other hand, I can still feel the sweetness and beauty of the world I had been in – being with you."

MAY 13, 1972: RACHELI

You canceled your plans so as to come here sooner. To come to me earlier, as it's too hard to wait. My dear - I don't know what to say. Thanking you would only be stupid. Do you realize how happy you make me?

I'll be with you, I'll touch you, kiss you. I'll hold you – soon, much sooner than I ever hoped. I am so happy. I love you very much. I close my eyes and feel I'm in your arms, try to feel it too, my love.

The next day was momentous too: "Do you know what today's date – 14/5/72 means? It means I have exactly one more year to serve in the army. A year from today I will be out." Then. . . my real life could start, and already I knew that David would be part of it.

My dream-plan is to go to Europe for a few months after I get out of the army – with you. I have for many years said to myself – I will go to Europe Someday with Somebody.

Things seem to be turning more and more real. I have an idea of the sum of days until that "someday" comes. And I also know something about a "somebody" I wish to go with. Hey – I seem to be getting old, and childish dreams are turning into plans and schedules.

MAY 13, 1972: DAVID

Even though I loved Racheli's letters written in English, I had to tell her that her letters in Hebrew -- and especially her love letters – made an even more profound impression: "Maybe it's because

Hebrew is a more poetic language than English or maybe it's because you are more of a poet than you give yourself credit for."

And I was equally impressed by how she pulled off an "Alice's Restaurant" (Arlo Guthrie's 20-minute talking blues satire against the Vietnam War draft) in getting herself out of the officer's training course. I passed the letter around and Ken Bob, a close friend and member of the RJU -- and later the president of the Labor Zionist organization Ameinu -- said sardonically: "Where did that girl learn to be so disrespectful of authority? It's just terrible!" I had to ask the same question:

> *Maybe you've been reading too many subversive books: Catch-22, Slaughterhouse 5 (hey, I've got another one that I'm going to send to you: One Flew Over the Cuckoo's Nest). As to your writing dirty jokes on the test (what are you trying to do, corrupt the purity of the Israeli army?), it's clear what you've got on your mind. I'm so happy that you won't have to be an officer (I really think I would have trouble making love to an Israeli officer; look what happened to Portnoy!).*

MAY 16, 1972: RACHELI

I received David's letter about the demonstration against the war in Vietnam and I also heard on the radio about the attempt to assassinate George Wallace. But these events seemed far away, because on the very same day:

> *All of Israel was holding her breath when we heard about the plane captured by the terrorists and it felt like a national holiday when the plane was taken over by the IDF. Because everyone is involved in some way – one of the boys from Kfar Ruppin was almost among the men who took the plane.*

The Sabena Airline plane had been hijacked on May 8 by Black September and forced to land at Israel's Lod Airport. An Israeli commando unit, the Sayeret Matkal, in which two Kfar Ruppin boys served, stormed the plane, freeing all 90 passengers and killing the two male Black September members and capturing the two females. It was a moment of great trauma and triumph for Israel and the sense of national unity was palpable. It seemed to me there was an unbridgeable gap between this sense of unity and the chasm in American society between those who supported and those who opposed the Vietnam War.

MAY 15, 1972: DAVID

It suddenly occurred to me that it was nearly two years since we started corresponding and one year since we were writing to each other several times a week:

> *Whether we like it or not (and I hope we like it), all these letters really add up to a real relationship, at least in the sense that even when we're not together, you have become an inseparable part of my life. To put it more simply, I love you.*

In the last period, my letter writing had become somewhat less frequent, for which I apologized. I was now in the home stretch before the master's exam. I had just gotten the bad news that I had to write the exam in pen and not on a typewriter: "you know how bad my handwriting is ... Well, as Kurt Vonnegut would say, 'so it goes.'"

MAY 18, 1972: RACHELI

Having spent the full week of my vacation in bed at home, sick with German measles, I should have been grumpy. But on the last day, the news of my next deployment came and it was good!

> *I'm going to a Nachal settlement called Mitzpe Shalem. This place is in the Jordan Valley, near the Dead Sea. It's not actually on the shore but a few kilometers in the mountains that go down to the sea. I hear from everyone who had been there it's the most beautiful place in the Jordan Valley.*
> *And, it's really close to Jerusalem. About an hour, no more.*
> *So – this is really good news.*

Once I got to Mitzpe, as we called it, it turned out even better: there was a direct bus from Jerusalem. The bus would drop you off at the junction with the main road that skirted the Dead Sea. From there you would call up on the field telephone to the outpost perched on the plateau about 400 meters above the road, and hope the telephone operator could line up a ride for you, either someone due back from a trip or an army vehicle sent down specially to fetch you. If no rides were to be had, it was a 1.5-mile hike up the lunarscape barren hills. In the course of my nearly year of service at Mitzpe I did the trek on foot twice: once during the day and another on a beautiful moon-lit night. The latter, especially, was magical, although long and arduous.

MAY 18, 1972, THURSDAY AFTERNOON (HANDWRITTEN): DAVID

I'm sitting in my office waiting for non-existent students to come hear non-pearls of wisdom about Jewish history.

At noon, I finished the Master's exam and, boy, am I glad it's over. It was just terrible – an enormous piece of shit (excuse the Hebrew). First of all, I didn't sleep much last night, but that hardly bothered me. The main problem was the questions:

1. What is the role of bias in writing history? Can "objective" history be written? Discuss, in relation to a left or right-wing movement in the 20th Century.

On this one, I totally screwed up. I wrote this superficial essay on different interpretations of Nazism, but then couldn't come to a conclusion about "objective" history. That's a really dumb question, but the others were even harder, so I chose this one to destroy myself on.

2. Discuss the role of agriculture and agricultural classes in political and economic developments during the industrial revolution.

I did better on this one, talking about Russia and France. If I pass the exam, it will be on the strength of this answer.

Anyway, as Bob (Dylan) Zimmerman says: "20 years of school and they put you on the day shift."

MAY 20, 1972: DAVID

At last, I gave Racheli a break from academic bulletins. It was Shavu'ot, the holiday celebrating the giving of the Torah, and the RJU held a festive meal followed by a *tikkun* (all-night study session) at the Hillel House that started with studying the Book of Ruth. A great change of pace from the triumphs and tragedies of European history. I had a sudden realization that what counted in studying was not the subject matter – history, Tanakh – but just the fact of studying. This is what I was looking forward to for the next year at the Hebrew University: study for its own sake without exams or degrees.

Our tikkun culminated in the early hours of the morning with a talk by Zalman Schachter, who had already acquired quite a reputation as a spokesman for Jewish renewal, a "neo-Hasidic rabbi: Orthodox yet quite radical." He argued that the historical Torah consisting of laws was not given on Shavu'ot, as Jewish tradition believes, but on Yom Kippur. The Torah of Shavu'ot was not a body of laws, but instead a Torah of cyclical time that is revealed to Jews every year and that relates to the problems of our own time in a "sort of Buberian dialogue with God." The problem with Orthodoxy today is that it only follows the historical Torah given on Yom Kippur. Jewish Orthodoxy requires the Torah of Shavu'ot to infuse it with spiritual life. Schachter presented his ideas "in the usual Hasidic style, telling stories and giving *perushim* [interpretations] that were often illogically connected."

I was very impressed by all this, but, then:

He kind of ruined it by getting into a discussion with the audience at the end about messianism. The problem with his philosophy is that it is often quite abstract and leads to toleration of all sorts of kooky theories. For example, the idea of two Torahs is from the Kabbalah and forms the basis for some of the ideas of Shabbetai Zevi [the seventeenth-century failed Messiah]. So, there were some Jesus freaks who tried to fit their ideas into Schachter's and he didn't argue with them. There was also a guy who told us that we are all the Messiah. Most of the people got very impatient with all this garbage and the discussion sort of disintegrated. This all happened at 4 in the morning.

More or less par for the course for Judaism in Berkeley.

MAY 23, 1972: RACHELI

Somehow, despite the huge geographic distance and completely different realities we inhabited, there were moments of what felt like magical synchronicity.

It's 3:00 PM – I just read the letter of May 15 I got from you today. I found it amazing because there are some strikingly similar things I said yesterday and that you wrote in your letter today. Somehow it came to my mind yesterday that it's been almost two years since I first saw you. And I get a letter from you today - talking about the almost–two-years between us.

Letters like these were crucial in building our sense of mutual security that, once we were actually together, our lives would align, our times together would feel natural and beautiful, even though I was still going to be a soldier and he a student.

Needless to say, I was already jealous of the intellectual excitement David would experience as a visiting graduate student at the Hebrew University and I was nurturing some fantasies of occasionally sneaking into his classes and seminars as an unofficial auditor. And indeed, I did that as the academic year unfolded. The most memorable of his classes was the small seminar on Hebrew Literature with Professor Gershon Shaked, at the time one of the luminaries in the field. The seminar met in Shaked's home and, even though I am sure it was intellectually engaging, all I remember is how we laughed afterwards about the way he pronounced the English word "womb" – something like "voomp."

When I got David's letter the next day, announcing he'd taken his MA exam, I was delighted that the pressure cooker he'd been stewing in for weeks was finally taken off the burner. But, rather tongue-in-cheek, my primary reaction was: "I hope now you'll be able to devote more time to writing me. The truth is I would like you to sit all day long and just write me page after page. But – I would settle for twenty pages a day." In fact, I had no complaints: we had been writing almost every day and the only reason I had more than a day's stretch of no letters was the erratic delivery schedule of the IDF mail. Some days were barren, while others bore three letters in one batch.

And, willy-nilly, time was marching on and David's arrival was now within the scope of tolerable waiting:

> *Do you realize we will be together in a month and a half? It's great – I can hardly believe it. The 11th of July is a Tuesday, a day that God saw that "it is good" twice. [Genesis 1]. I hope I'll be able to get off for a few days – Tuesday till Sunday.*
>
> *Last night I couldn't help it – I kept thinking, dreaming of that Tuesday night together with you. It tasted like heaven.*

MAY 24, 1972: DAVID

I wrote that I had now reached a point in my life when I was ready to make a commitment. I had no need for further "experiences." But it was premature for us to make a commitment until we were together for a longer period of time:

> *Only when we have passed the point of exchanging information about our separate worlds, only when our individual worlds are completely shared can we start talking about a future together. I never told another girl "I love you" and I never felt as close to anyone else. I very much want to understand how you feel about kibbutz and I want you to understand how I feel about academic life, but I hope that our love takes priority over these things.*

MAY 27, 1972: DAVID

While our earlier ideological debates had taken a back seat to romance, they weren't entirely gone. Having gotten past my Master's exam, I now returned to the discussion of kibbutz, which had been the subject of an intense conversation during my March visit when we had sat on the hill in Kfar Ruppin overlooking the Jordan River. My thoughts were perhaps no more coherent now, but I wanted to develop the idea of the kibbutz as what is called today an "intentional" community. It was an "unnatural" community in that the members were all there as a result of conscious choice, and that kind of social organization could only work as a result of ideological consciousness. But then things got more complicated for children of the kibbutz founders like Racheli herself, who were born there and for whom it was, at least to some degree, natural. We were therefore in different places by virtue of our origins. For me, the decision to live on a kibbutz meant "a revolutionary decision in a very personal sense; it means a complete change in lifestyle and in attitude toward occupation." If I were ever to make that revolutionary decision, I wrote, it would be because Racheli brought me to that consciousness.

MAY 28, 1972, MIDNIGHT: RACHELI

I finally arrived at Mitzpe Shalem and immediately sent a letter that night, eager to share my first impressions:

Generally, the place here seems very nice and the view is breathtakingly beautiful. The place is very high up, the slopes are steep. It seems to me almost hanging over the Dead Sea water.

I found out I can have you visit me here almost any time. There's a bus from Jerusalem at 12:45 PM.

I counted myself very lucky given the natural beauty, the daily Jerusalem bus and the liberal visitors' policies for the "brass." The poor, lowly soldiers were only allowed visitors on infrequent visitors' days. I also felt that this posting did not conflict with my political principles: the spot where Mitzpe was planted, atop the rocky Judean Hills, was so isolated and barren that I was sure it would never be converted from an army outpost, with its legitimate security function overlooking the border with Jordan, to a civilian settlement. Thus, I could feel good about not contributing to the settlement project of

Israel's far-right and religious parties. I was wrong, of course. Four years after my stint there, Mitzpe was converted into a kibbutz and relocated from the hilltop to the wide Dead Sea basin, where date palms and vegetables could grow in the salty soil. So much for my political savvy.

But, without that foreknowledge, I could really throw myself into the settlement's life, and working in the vegetable fields felt like a home-coming. My duties as one of two female NCO's at Mitzpe were varied. The actual military obligations were minimal: mostly a daily ten-minute roll call for all the female soldiers when my co-NCO and I inspected their rooms for cleanliness and order, their rifles for sand particles, and their army fatigues for obvious stains and wrinkles. More important, and much more rewarding, was my role as an informal social worker, helping the girls with issues with their families at home, getting along with their comrades and, most commonly, boyfriend troubles. It was a natural progression from my work as a youth movement counselor and the seeds for my eventual career as a psychotherapist.

There was also secretarial work in the office, which I loathed. I was even trained for that: "Yesterday morning I went to Tel Aviv for a day's course in secretary work for the settlement. I'm allergic to that kind of work." But I was fortunate: "Luckily, we have a girl here who does all of that, so I hope not to have work in the office." Of course, what I considered real work was in the fields or the small jewelry and leather goods workshop, and occasionally a shift in the communal kitchen and dining room. Anything I got to do with my hands I valued and found rewarding – my kibbutz upbringing had primed me for that.

But the most interesting work emerged a few weeks after my arrival. One morning at breakfast I noticed an old man lining up with the soldiers and loading his tray with vegetables, yogurt and eggs. He looked to be 80 years old, with Ben Gurion-like shocks of wild white hair at his temples (in fact, he was 65, three years younger than I am as of this writing!). He was wearing rumpled work clothes, like those men on my kibbutz had worn during my childhood in the 1950's. He held a pipe in his left hand and carried the tray of food in his right. On the edge of his tray lay a rusty trowel.

He was Pesach Bar Adon, a famous archaeologist, who was living with us at Mitzpe as a permanent guest so he could pursue excavations in the surrounding hills. He mostly found remains of prehistoric habitation: stone circles marking spots where "homes" had been, with stone tools found scattered about. Pesach rejoiced with finding every stone hammer, serrated blade, or arrowhead, but what he was really looking for, I realized after I read up on him, was a second "Cave of the Treasure." He had uncovered one in 1961 in Nachal Mishmar, only twenty kilometers south of us. It contained strange copper figures that may have been part of a prehistoric cult. They are now in the Israel Museum. It stood to reason there would be more, though nothing like it had been found by anyone else. Pesach had been looking for over a decade, a lone man scouring the desert for treasures.

Pesach during the Cave of the Treasure excavations

He was delighted to hear that I was interested in archaeology. I mentioned that my mother had worked with Yigael Yadin at Masada. A cloud passed over his eyes, "Eh… crazy mass suicide," he let slip. He had never received the publicity and admiration lavished on Yadin and Masada. Perhaps this was so because the mysterious objects he found testified to a highly sophisticated material culture of a lost civilization predating the Hebrews by millennia, which was of no use for the heroic Israeli national narrative.

Pesach was taken aback when I asked what I needed to do to qualify to work with him. "Just come," he smiled, "I start at dawn; the early light is excellent for discerning unusual contours in the earth." I did, and between hewn rocks and stone tools we talked about everything, from archaeology to America. We became good friends and I introduced David to him when he arrived. We visited Pesach a number of times in his small, spartan apartment in Jerusalem. He cooked us a memorable dinner on an army-issued kerosene field stove dating back to the 1948 war. The meager fried eggs and sardines remain one of the best meals I've ever had. The walls of his apartment were lined with shelves crammed with stacks of used cigarette packs. He was a chain smoker and each empty cardboard pack became a "drawer" for the artifacts he found. A few pieces were too big, so shoe boxes held those, but mostly it was layer upon layer of cigarette packs. We continued to visit Pesach in Jerusalem after I left Mitzpe in early 1973. It was a lovely friendship but I think he was a bit jealous: he gave no reason at all, let alone a convincing one, why he couldn't come to our wedding.

I quickly became enchanted with Mitzpe, enjoying swimming in the Dead Sea and hiking in the local wadis, but the best part was having a semi-private room, shared with Ma'ayan, the other NCO. It was all my own on weekends when she went home. I was already daydreaming about David spending Shabbat there with me and that's exactly what he did. We also had a field telephone in our room, which I could actually answer while in bed! That supplied another focus for lovely fantasies, especially when compared to the ordeal of receiving a call from David in Kfar Ruppin. And, in fact, once David got to Jerusalem, I supplied him with a made-up Israeli soldier's ID number. He would call me almost every day from a public pay phone in the Commercial Center of Kiryat Yovel, using that number in order to gain access to the IDF's own phone system.

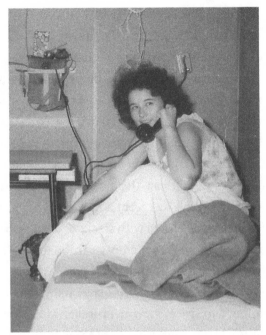

On the telephone in my room
at Mitzpe, May, 1972

MAY 29, 1972: DAVID

Our return to ideological subjects created a paradoxical development. While earlier, broaching the question of a romance, not to speak of sexual relations, seemed the hardest thing to put into words, it was now these matters that vexed me.

The intellectual part might become the hardest. It didn't become hard because you are any less intellectual than I am (you aren't), but because we were probably afraid of disagreeing. It means as much to me to be able to share my intellectual struggles with you as being with you emotionally. In a way, I feel like when we have a really good discussion, it's like making love in a different way.

Fortunately, not everything was intellectual:

Yesterday, I went on a hike with the hevre in the Santa Cruz mountains. We hiked for about 16 km in the most beautiful country: the redwood trees were so high you could barely see the tops. The air was heavy and warm, and smelled of the sweet smell of wet soil, and moss, and pine trees. We carried bread and cheese, and oranges and wine, and ate our lunch beside a lovely waterfall. In a paradoxical way, I felt happy and complete, yet I also missed you very much. I wanted to be walking with you and feel you squeeze my hand, wordless in this most beautiful place in the world.

From nature back to politics. There was a coda to the big demonstrations against Nixon's war:

Here's something to show you how radical your good-for-nothing boyfriend is. The following news appeared in an article in Rolling Stone (the national magazine of the "counter-culture"):

"In protest against Nixon's war policy, Berkeley returned to its active self. On Tuesday, a rally of some three thousand people was held on Sproul Plaza.

'Organize and work against the war,' said one speaker.

'General strike,' someone yelled in reply from the back of the crowd."

What the article didn't mention was who yelled the last remark. You guess it: I did. That's what you get for studying history: it so happened that, at the time, I was reading about General Strikes in France at the beginning of the twentieth century. Unfortunately, no one in the crowd knew what I was saying. I wasn't calling for a student strike, but for a labor strike. Still, it's pretty funny that my silly remark ended up in a national magazine.

JUNE 1, 1972: DAVID

Our Berkeley Jewish community was in shock. Three Japanese terrorists had attacked the arrivals hall of Israel's Lod Airport and killed twenty-six people, including Aharon Katzir, one of Israel's most eminent scientists. This horrible massacre had been brought home to us because Katzir's daughter, Yael, was a graduate student in anthropology at Berkeley and we were quite friendly with her. Katzir himself had taught at Berkeley. A memorial service was scheduled on the campus for the next day. We might have been debating "Israel versus Galut," but we were all so deeply invested in Israel that an event like this struck us personally.

JUNE 5, 1972: RACHELI

Strangely, there is no mention of the Lod Airport massacre in my letters. I have no recollection or explanation for this lacuna. I also made no mention that the date of my letter was the fifth anniversary of the beginning of the Six Day War. Most Israelis were still in the post-victory euphoric state and the anniversary was marked with many commemorations, photo books, and popular songs. I am sure there was some kind of event at Mitzpe Shalem and it's likely I was involved in supervising the soldiers who prepared a program of some sort. But it is a total blank in my memory. Perhaps I had consigned it to oblivion because I already had mixed feelings. I certainly shared the general sentiment of wonder at the lightning speed of Israel's victory and relief that Kfar Ruppin was fortunate in not losing any of our men in the war. But I was already agnostic about the war's consequences; the occupation of Arab territories seized during the war already loomed large as Israel's long-term quagmire.

But perhaps the simplest explanation for my silence was simply that David's impending arrival filled every inch of my heart, every nook in my mind. It was just thirty-six days until we would be reunited, but our letter writing would end much sooner: "I just realized – in less than three weeks you'll leave Berkeley. Which means after that there won't be any address to mail my love to, would there?" I proposed writing a letter or two care of Shelly, David's friend in London, if he could provide the dates he'd be there and the address. Other than that, we would have a period of about ten days with no communication, especially as the mail to Mitzpe was particularly slow. I apologized: "

We don't have a Mobile Post so the mail has to be brought to
Jericho. There is not always a car going down there, so that mail

is not sent out and brought every day. Be prepared then, for my
letters to take ten or even more days to reach you.

But those would be the last ten days of our separation, so I could
see getting through them without much difficulty, since I had his
beautiful letters to accompany me:

You have such an amazing ability to make me happy. You make
me love you so much, want you so much. When you write me
letters like these, I can really feel our love growing; feel how you
feel, my love, how you make me more able to love you.

I felt very good after writing you that letter about next year. But
I felt a thousand times happier when I read your letter about
making a commitment, completing my hopes into something so
perfect and beautiful, it is divine.

JUNE 5, 1972: DAVID

I announced to Racheli that I had purchased a joint present for
us: a water bed (that fad is by now long gone, only useful in movies
evoking the 1970s). I had slept on one when I visited New York back
in February and found it more comfortable than a regular bed and
"I've been told that it is really great for making love (that remains to
be seen)." I planned to send it to Israel, get a hold of some lumber to
build a frame and set it up in my Jerusalem apartment for the next
year. I somehow managed to do this, but the novelty wore off and
the supposed benefit for love-making proved utterly false – much
too bouncy! We left it in Racheli's parents' attic after our wedding.
It eventually went the way of all water beds.

JUNE 7, 1972: DAVID

Very good news! I passed my master's exam!!!! It wasn't exactly a
distinguished pass: I got a B+ but they didn't give very many A's.
I took my friend Fred out to dinner because he had helped me
study and, besides, we had made a bet: he would get a dinner off
me if I passed.

If memory serves, we went to the Heidelberg Café where we had originally met the previous fall and had huge corn beef sandwiches in honor – or mockery – of my Master's exam essay on German history.

JUNE 10, 1972: RACHELI

"You know, my love," I began, "it's already 1:00 AM. So, it's already tomorrow and the date on my watch has already changed to the 11th. I may, then, whisper to myself before I fall asleep: another month, just one more month." I was becoming giddy with anticipation; waiting a whole month seemed almost unbearable:

Maybe it seems so long since you left because I have been fighting very hard with enormous desire for you. Because not like any time before, I know all the little details, the light touches and sounds, your eyes, your warm lips, the softness, the great desire and satisfaction. That is what I miss so terribly every moment.

My imagination was turbo-charged: a young brain in love.

However, I needed to make a confession:

There's this one guy here, maybe I am a little attracted to him. We fooled around a bit [I was not aware then that the idiomatic meaning of this expression is sexual], talking and joking.

But I am sure it was just a stupid sudden feeling. Maybe it is because knowing you attract someone else is somehow a compliment that makes you happy to respond in a way that will keep the game going. David, my dear, you can be perfectly sure there is absolutely nothing. But if I hadn't made this clear (and made more of it than there really was) I would have a tiny, still painful spot. I love you very much and I feel completely filled up by you – by my love for you.

Maybe what I told you about was some kind of test – but it was a very easy one.

My trepidation about this confession – and the rather innocent moments that occasioned it – was unnecessary, as David reassured me in response. And, perhaps, I was helped by the fact that a few days later this guy left Mitzpe, having completed his tour of duty there.

JUNE 12, 1972: DAVID

My friend and fellow student, Jeremy Popkin, who would go on to a distinguished career as a French historian, called me up and said that he was having trouble with a paper he was writing. So, I dropped whatever I was doing and went over to his apartment where we spent three hours trying to solve his problem. "This gave me a very good feeling: that my opinion is valuable, that I can solve historical problems, and, most important, that we have a sort of intellectual community in which we help each other." This was not an isolated moment, but, rather, a harbinger of my academic career. Over the years, I have found this kind of collaborative work the most rewarding. Perhaps this was something I learned from my experience on kibbutz and in the Radical Jewish Union, that intellectuals should not work as solitary animals.

There was much to do before I left Berkeley. Nevertheless, I was determined to take at least one more hike in the Berkeley Hills with their beautiful brown shingle houses. Little could I have imagined that, fourteen years later, I would move to a brown shingle house in those very hills and remain there until today.

JUNE 17, 1972: RACHELI

I think this is going to be the last letter I write you because I won't be able to write all through next week and after that you'll be too close to Israel to be reached. I won't be able to write next week because I will be in "mailless" territory – I'm going to Sinai for a week!!!

I was sure the week-long trip would help pass the letter-less period more easily. I was very excited just writing about it:

A few guys from Mitzpe Shalem plus a few other friends who're getting out of the army now are having a trip to celebrate FREEDOM. And – they've taking the female NCO's along - why not – I'll be getting out in only eleven months.

We're going in two command-cars, food, gas and everything taken

through "friends" in all sorts of places in the army. There'll be
around 12 of us and it will have to be FANTASTIC!
As you can see – I'm doing my share of guarding my country and
my people very carefully.

The Sinai trip was, indeed fabulous:

The great thing about it was that we went to all those God-
forgotten places very far off any main road, where a normal car
could not get through. Also, we visited a lot of Bedouins and, as
there were three people who spoke Arabic well, heard a lot of
interesting stories, were invited for coffee, and told of beautiful,
undiscovered wadis in the area.

The most exhilarating place was the top of a mountain on a wide,
high plateau, totally empty as far as the eye could see, where a lone
Bedouin invited us for coffee in his "home," a tiny lean-to tent, in a
place he said was called "The End of the World."

I thought this letter was my last, so I ended by anticipating our
embrace upon David's arrival at the Haifa harbor. That seemed much
more romantic than landing at Lod Airport's drab runway. It also
resonated with my parents' first arrival in Haifa on November 24,
1940 - only to be deported to Mauritius just over a fortnight later -
and my mother's return in August, 1945. My mother disembarked
the ship and, within a few days, would jump into the arms of the
man, dashing in his British soldier's uniform, who would become my
father. Now, it was my turn: "I picture myself waiting at the docks,
you're coming in from the boat, you open your arms and kiss me -
and then – Heaven."

JUNE 19, 1972: DAVID

I received two letters from Racheli on the very last day that mail
would come to my Berkeley address. The most important subject
in the letters was the account of her flirtation with her company
commander in Mitzpe Shalem. This made me very happy for several
reasons. First, the fact that she felt so secure in our relationship to

tell me about her feelings. Second, it made me think of the attraction I had had earlier in the year to the woman named Debbie, which I had related to Racheli because I felt that it would strengthen our bond if I could be honest about such things. Resisting a relationship with Debbie had also felt like a test, which I had to pass in order to be even more secure in my love. I felt so sure that I had even added, half-jokingly, "by the way, she will be in Jerusalem next year, so you can meet her and see if I made the right decision." Now, Racheli had met and passed a similar test.

And there was more:

But aside from that, it made it me happy in another way. I think I would be positively insulted if other men didn't find you attractive. You know, in the shtetl, Orthodox women used to shave their heads after they married, so that they wouldn't be attractive to other men. I think that's ridiculous.

Leaving Berkeley was a bittersweet moment: the end of four intense, tumultuous years that had changed me in every way. But if this was my last letter, "then I am happy that all these hundreds of letters would end with a letter like this one. I don't think I've ever felt as clearly about our love."

JUNE 24, 1972: RACHELI

In the dozen letters and postcards David sent while on his trip, there was news of yet one more – and final – delay to July 19. We were delay-troopers by then, so I wasn't too upset. On June 24, I realized that, given the postponement, I could try to get yet one more letter into his hands in London.

I just got the letter from you saying you will be coming 8 days later. Of course, waiting another eight days seems now like almost forever, but that doesn't matter. . . It's great to be able to write you again – I sort of fell mute – getting all those beautiful letters and not being able to talk back to you. I have to hurry and get this to the mail. I hold my breath waiting to have you.

JULY 1, 1972: RACHELI

July 1st seemed like it would have been the natural point to bring the letter-writing to a close, but we were both determined to squeeze every last drop out of this stage of our love, so David suggested I write him at the American Express office in Athens, a common practice at the time when you had no local address. He would spend a few days there before boarding the boat to Israel on July 17.

I think that my major worry has always been that our relationship is not real by itself, but is, rather, an escape from facing loneliness with no lover in reality. There was perhaps some hidden thought that all this was really built up in the air. There was nothing solid over a long period of time - to hang onto, to be some kind of proof. And now you're on your way – to me. This is what it is – more than anything else – you're coming to me, to hold me in your arms, for me to kiss you.

I'm counting the days. I used to count the months, then the weeks. Counting the days should make the rest of the time we still have to wait very short. It doesn't. Because my mind is switched to counting days. Seventeen days suddenly are much more than a little over two weeks.

And, tongue-in-cheek, I complained in a corny way about the Almond Joy candy bar David had confessed that he had forgotten to pack: "I'm, of course, terribly sad about the Almond Joy. I will not have the joy of tasting it. But the sweetness of your kisses will make up for it."

I told David that as I was writing the letter, I was listening to Beethoven's Violin Concerto, an intense emotional experience that made me miss him very much. This piece, in particular, moved me greatly, as it brought back the vivid memory of a concert I attended in my senior year in high school, hearing Isaac Stern play it with the Israel Philharmonic. It was at Kibbutz Ein Gev across the Sea of Galilee from my high school, where a classmate snuck me into the concert hall and to a center seat in the fourth row! My parents attended the concert too, but as proper paying customers. Speaking with my mother afterwards, we marveled at the sweet sound and she said "it was as sweet as the pleasure of love-making." I agreed whole-heartedly, although at the time I had no idea what that pleasure was. My mother gave me a momentary quizzical look and mumbled, "hmmm…" I carried those words with me until I learned, with David, just what my mother was talking about.

JUNE 21 OR 22, 1972 – SOMEWHERE IN THE AIR [HANDWRITTEN ON THE PLANE TO ENGLAND]: DAVID

To my most dear beloved,

Somehow, with scarcely looking behind me, I left Berkeley, got on a plane and am almost halfway to you. The story of my departure is itself something. I got a call the day before saying that my flight was to leave at 5:00 pm instead of 10:30 pm. As my stuff was hardly packed, I got mad at the guy who called. He told me that it was lucky we were going at all because the airline we were supposed to go on went BANKRUPT last Friday! Isn't that amazing. Luckily, they found another plane or else I'd still be sitting in 2412 Atherton. In spite of all the enormous hassle, I somehow made it. Perhaps, because of it, I barely noticed that I was leaving – I still don't really realize it. Last night, we had a wonderful party - all my friends came and said goodbye. It was quite sentimental, especially parting with my friend, Fred, who has been a close friend on so many levels this year.

We are coming in to land in England … Last time I landed here (only 3 months ago!) it was also on my way to you – but what a difference!

JULY 6 OR 7, 1972: RACHELI

I wrote my last letter to David in Hebrew, as I had done throughout the nearly two years of letter-writing when I wanted to convey particularly intense emotions, when I wanted soaring, poetic language to capture a momentous day. The *last letter* certainly felt like a huge milestone.

It's strange. The end of such a long road. Very long, and narrow and twisting. The three weeks we were together over Passover were some kind of leap - to a different world. Sometimes it seems to me it was a dream world. But more and more I do believe that it was actually a leap into a real world – into the wide, well-lit, and wonderous road that we'll be walking on, hand in hand, so soon. There is something wonderous and fabulous and grand – more than anything I had dreamed of, and wanted and knew – that is hidden in you, inside you.

And there is something wonderous hidden inside me – you know what it is? The love - with such great abundance, and life, and beauty – and it's all for you. It's yours, my love.

I am all yours.

"I am my beloved's and my beloved is mine – who grazes among the roses." [Song of Songs 2:16]. Thus, it has already been said – everything, whole, perfect.

And I kiss you, my beloved.

JUNE 22 – JULY 19, 1972: DAVID

I stayed for my first week in Europe with my friends, Shelly and Debbie Schreter and then went to meet my parents for the first days of July in Amsterdam. Together, we returned to England and undertook a four-day trip to Scotland. They then returned to America, while I spent some more time in London and then made my way south to Athens where I took a boat to Israel, arriving on July 19. I wrote frequently during that nearly four-week period, detailed reports about my travels and expressions of longing. As I had often done in the past, I turned to poetry to let my heart speak:

When you are old and grey and full of sleep
And nodding by the fire, take down this book

And slowly read, and dream of the soft look
Your eyes had once, and of their shadows deep.

How many loved your moments of glad grace
And loved your beauty with love false or true
But one man loved the pilgrim soul in you
And loved the sorrows of your changing face.

And bending down beside the glowing bars
Murmur a little sadly how love fled
And paced upon the mountains overhead
And hid his face amid a crowd of stars.

--W. B. Yeats

When I was young at Harvard some four years ago, I remember reading that poem and loving it and loving the girl it was written to and wondering if I would ever love a girl with a "pilgrim soul." I was a romantic then and wanted love to be a mixture between happiness and sadness, memory and desire. I wanted the girl I loved to be above the ordinary, to guard a mysterious secret inside her (the secret of why we are here?), which I could only discover in those gentle minutes between night and morning, communicated by a silent embrace.

I wanted love to be something that would make life new and make the everyday holy. I am afraid of the future, afraid of life ending, mostly afraid of life slipping like water through my fingers. Somehow, four hands are better than two at catching the water and holding it, if for a brief moment.

In the four years since I read that poem, much of the romanticism had vanished – the moments of magic seemed to grow fewer and fewer; realism secured my life like a vise.

Then, quite when I least expected it, you came and the magic slowly began to return. To me, as I know you more and more, you are the most beautiful woman in the world. I love you because you don't take anything for granted, because each moment is special, each flower beautiful. I love you because you know how to take a step back from life and sense what is somehow divine and inexplicable about our existence. And you know how to do that without leaving reality.

Your letter that I got today has not left me; I have read it many times, but can't really express how I feel. It is hard and frightening to think of the future. It goes beyond just "making plans" and involves grasping at something mysterious, even religious. It certainly goes beyond words like these.

You know, my dearest, when it comes time to make a decision, we will know without saying a word what it should be. Either we will be so much in love that there will be no choice or it will be clear the other way. That is my naïve romanticism. It somehow goes beyond all the petty and sordid stupidities of a "relationship." One has to work hard at it, but the work is only worth it if there is a divine spark underneath. We have to search for that rare combination of words and touches, intellect and emotions. I know that I have more confidence in you than in anyone else in the world that you know how to find it.

This, then, is my last letter to you. What can I say to end nearly two years of letters? Racheli, my love, I want very, very much to love you. I don't want love to hide "his face amid a crowd of stars." I want it here with you. I want the prose of these last years to become poetry.
David

And now that we are both "old and grey and full of sleep," we are writing this book to remind us of how our love began. And how we hold it tight until the day when it, too, alas, will "hide its face amid a crowd of stars."

WHERE OUR CHILDREN ARE

DAVID ARRIVED IN ISRAEL on July 19, 1972 and moved into an apartment in Jerusalem. As we had hoped, while he was attending classes at the Hebrew University and Racheli continued to serve at Mitzpe Shalem, we saw each other every week and spoke on the phone almost daily. As the year unfolded, we began planning to go to the US for David to do his PhD in Jewish history and for Racheli her BA. Racheli wanted to recapture the intellectual excitement of her year in Newton, Massachusetts in an American university. And David, for all that he enjoyed his studies at the Hebrew University, felt that Israeli academia was not the place he could make his greatest contribution (much later he would be pleasantly surprised at the great interest Israeli scholars and students expressed in his work).

In December, Racheli was in Jerusalem on leave and in the early morning hours told David something her mother, Anina, had said to her: if we planned to get married, perhaps we should do so in Israel before leaving, because kibbutz members were not automatically allowed to travel abroad. David looked at Racheli for the blink of an eye and said: "Well, that settles it. If she says we should get married, let's do it." We woke up our friend, Ken Bob, who was staying the night, and he toasted us with orange juice.

On March 20, 1973, we married in Kfar Ruppin, with Chaim Druckman, the rabbi who had dropped in to visit Racheli in the Communa in Ramat Gan, officiating. We didn't know at the time that Druckman was already active in the nascent settler movement and the following year would be one of the founders and spiritual leaders of Gush Emunim. Later still, he became a Knesset member from the far-right Tehiya Party. It was quite hard to reconcile the warm, generous, charismatic teacher who seemed so open to secular audiences, with the extremist politician. And it was embarrassing after the wedding when everybody in Kfar Ruppin referred to Druckman as "Racheli's rabbi."

After spending a little over a month on the kibbutz (during which time Racheli was formally released from the army), we went to Europe, starting in Greece and ending in London. That summer, we worked with RJU friends, including Ken Bob, at a Habonim summer camp in the Catskills for campers who had just finished eleventh grade. At the end of the summer, we arrived in Los Angeles to begin our studies and our journey together as a married couple. And, so it was that our epistolary romance reached its conclusion or, better, opened a new chapter, when our love would grow for over half a century.

In our first ten years in the United States, we twice came close to living Israel, first on kibbutz and then in Haifa. As we already described, we were among the founders of a garin to Kibbutz Gezer, but several visits to the kibbutz convinced us that it wasn't for us. In 1983, we spent a half a year in Haifa where David received a job offer at the university. To say that we did not fall in love with the city would be an understatement. And even though David very much enjoyed teaching the Israeli students in Hebrew, he found the atmosphere of the university stifling and contentious.

At the time, we were living in Binghamton, New York, which was also hardly the Promised Land. We find it hard to imagine what our lives would have been like if we had stayed there, although the two families we bonded most strongly with remain close friends to this day. Fortuitously, a job came open in Berkeley and we were able to complete one circle of our lives by returning to this magical place.

Some of the keys to this turn of events should already be obvious from our letters: David's love for Berkeley, a place where he feels most himself, a love that Racheli already intuitively felt from her first visit there. Yet we can't pretend that the decision not to live in Israel was an easy or obvious one, especially for Racheli, who had to come to terms with her family living ten thousand miles away. It only really sunk in for her how difficult it was for her mother, who had left her own parents at around the same age, never to see them again. and for her father who had similarly left his mother, when in the 1990's she read her mother's diary entry from December 10, 1939 – the day she left her family standing on the platform at the main train station in Prague. Although there were times early on when that decision created a certain tension with Racheli's parents and brothers, they came to accept and embrace the American branch of the family.

A repeated refrain in our early letters was: "Do you know where your children are?" Early on, when we decided to stay in America, we harbored a fear that if our children were born and raised in the United States, they would not have the connection to Judaism, kibbutz and Israel that has been so essential to who we are. We can safely say now that that fear was misplaced. As a result of spending a sabbatical year at Kfar Ruppin in 1992-1993 and of many visits to Israel before and after, our children know very much where *they* are: deeply connected to family and friends in Israel and with a sense of their Jewish identities firmly held, each in his or her own way, even as they reach out in their marriages and friendships to a wider world.

With our children, summer 1986

And we, too, feel those deep connections just as vividly today as we did back then. In the intervening fifty years, at least for us, America and Israel have grown closer together. We have a common language with family and friends over there, even though ten thousand miles still separate us. Their joys and sorrows are ours, and ours are theirs. We commiserate with them about the decline and vicissitudes of their country and they commiserate with us about ours. It is that human connection, rather than some abstract ideology, that seems most important to us now. As Hannah Arendt wisely said: "I don't love a people; I love my friends."

We think of ourselves as secular, non-believers in things supernatural. After all, both of our fathers were hardheaded scientists and we ourselves are still rationalists, albeit discouraged ones. But in journeying back fifty years to when we met and fell in love, it seems to us, in a sense, fated – *bashert* is the almost untranslatable Yiddish word for it – that we should have found each other. In our late adolescence, we were both on parallel tracks, even if in very different geographical and cultural locations. David's year in Israel in 1958-1959 and Racheli's year in the United States in 1967-1968 were the temporary immersions into each other's cultures that made it possible for our parallel tracks to intersect.

There were other factors as well. Racheli's teacher Ehud ("Uda") Luz ignited her interest in Jewish thought, something exceedingly rare among kibbutzniks of her generation. And while David's path to a Jewish awakening – summer camps and the Radical Jewish Union in Berkeley – was perhaps less idiosyncratic, it was not at all obvious that he would marry his career as an intellectual to the study of Jewish history. We met at the moment when we had both become so deeply engaged in these subjects that we felt as if we had each met our alter-ego.

In a deeper sense, our trajectories toward each other were, at least partially, set by the journeys of our parents that we described in the prologues to this book. David's father had in common with Racheli's parents the crucible of the socialist Zionist youth movement in their teenage years. While he never made it to the kibbutz that was the goal of his movement, the values by which he lived were the fruit of that experience: love of nature, embrace of manual labor and a fierce belief in the equality of human beings. The Zionism of our parents was anything but nationalistic: it represented the desire to create a humane Jewish society and to realize utopian dreams of a collective life.

The debates about Zionism and kibbutz that recur repeatedly in our letters seem now to be echoes of our parents' ideals. Yet our grappling with these issues took place at an historical moment when Israel and the kibbutz were beginning to metamorphose into something very different from those ideals. Our dreams were already haunted by disillusionment, as, indeed, were the dreams of our parents.

Writing this memoir has been an unexpected adventure. We have traveled back to visit our younger selves and embraced them – sometimes innocent, sometimes arrogant, often verbose and self-important -- for laying the foundation for the people we have become. Have we lived up to the ideals we expressed to each other fifty years ago? Not entirely, at least, not as we imagined them then. The world has certainly not lived up to them. But instead of lamenting that sad reality, we treasure living the lives we have chosen to live.

ACKNOWLEDGEMENTS

WE ARE GRATEFUL to a wide circle of friends who read and commented on early versions of this book. First and foremost, our children Noam and Tali, who assured us that it didn't make them cringe and marveled at getting to know us at such young ages, so much younger and more naïve than they are today.

Fred Rosenbaum (whom you met in the preface and elsewhere in the book) was our first reader and the one who suggested the joint memoir format for our project. Our friend of four decades, Chana Kronfeld, marked nearly every page with her legendary purple pen: comments, corrections, suggestions and appreciation. Muki Tzur wrote from Kibbutz Ein Gev on the shores of the Sea of Galilee with insightful reflections, memories of the time, and evocative connections to the kibbutz founders of the Second Aliyah, the subject of his lifelong research.

Many friends read the manuscript at different stages and offered enthusiastic support and helpful comments: Robert (Uri) Alter, Avner Ash, Christian Bailey, Heidi Berrin and Alan Shonkoff, Mario Biagioli, Ken Bob, Sara Bolder, Bradley Burston, David De

Nola, Bonny Fetterman, Susan Hamlin, Levi Kelman, Mark Linton, Molly McCarthy, Levana Mizrachi, Michel Nutkiewicz, Ilana Pardes, Jeremy Popkin, Steve Rosen, Sherman Rosenfeld, Susan and Al Adams, Andy Ross, Naomi Seidman, Shifra Sharlin, Marie-Brunette Spire, Sol Stern, Diane Wolf, Noam Zion, Steve Zipperstein, and all those whose names escape us at the moment.

Finally, we thanks Skyler Kratofil for expertly designing the paperback edition of this book.

ABOUT THE AUTHORS

RACHEL BIALE HAS WORKED as a therapist, parenting counselor, Jewish educator, cultural programmer and political organizer. She also writes and illuminates *ketubot* (Jewish marriage contracts). **David Biale** is the Emanuel Ringelblum Distinguished Professor of Jewish History at the University of California, Davis. He has also taught at Binghamton University and the Graduate Theological Union in Berkeley. They live in Berkeley, CA and have two children, Noam and Tali, and three grandchildren.

Other Books by Rachel Biale
Women and Jewish Law
Growing Up Below Sea Level: A Kibbutz Childhood
What Now? Two-Minute Tips for Solving Common Parenting Challenges

Other Books by David Biale
Gershom Scholem: Kabbalah and Counter-History
Power and Powerlessness in Jewish History

Eros and the Jews: From Biblical Israel to Contemporary America
Cultures of the Jews
Blood and Belief: The Circulation of a Symbol Between Jews and Christians
Not in the Heavens: The Tradition of Jewish Secular Thought
Hasidism: A New History
Gershom Scholem: Master of the Kabbalah

CPSIA information can be obtained
at www.ICGtesting.com
Printed in the USA
BVHW051017141022
649366BV00011BA/827